Workplace Bullying Lawyers' Guide

How to get more compen$ation for your client

Workplace Bullying Lawyers' Guide

How to get more compen$ation for your client

Kathryn-Magnolia Feeley

ℰ

Strategic Book Publishing and Rights Co.

Strategic Book Publishing and Rights Co.
12620 FM 1960, Suite A4-507
Houston TX 77065
www.sbpra.com

ISBN: 978-1-61897-986-5

Dedication

To my family

Contents

Acknowledgements

With grateful thanks to the Queensland Nurses' Union

About the author

Kathryn-Magnolia Feeley is a lawyer and Embassy legal strategist in Canberra, Australia. She was a guest speaker at the 2011 NSW Law Society Annual Conference on Litigation and Workplace Bullying and has lectured at the University of Canberra and the Australian National University.

Reviews

This is a very informative and exciting text, which speaks directly to the reader . . . I enjoyed the text as it is filled with medical information and practical advice: Smokeball peer review.

Kathryn-Magnolia Feeley provides invaluable direction and a practical framework (including precedents) to busy practitioners to enable them to quickly get to the crux of the client's legal issues and begin to map out a strategy—Owen Harris, Lawyer: BMath, GDMS, GDLP, JD.

This is a comprehensive and informative first-point for practitioners looking to expand their practice into the field. It is a valuable addition to any legal library.
Timothy Crispin: Barrister-at-Law ACT.

Disclaimer

This publication is available in jurisdictions worldwide. *The Workplace Bullying Lawyers' Guide* is intended to provide general information on workplace issues and does not constitute legal advice and the author Kathryn-Magnolia Feeley accepts no responsibility, or anyone associated with the publication, for the accuracy of material. People seeking advice on workplace bullying issues should seek advice from a lawyer in their particular area or jurisdiction.

Introduction

I wrote this guide for lawyers to get more compensation for their clients who were injured as a result of workplace bullying. References are from Australia, New Zealand, England, Ireland, Scotland, Sweden, European Union, Canada, and the United State of America and can be a point of reference for lawyers in other jurisdictions. Each legal argument is supported by legislation and case law for your submissions.

To succeed in litigating cases of injuries caused by workplace bullying, you must prove:

The injury was caused by the workplace
The nature of the actual injury

Investigate the workplace in question. The Private Group Investigators has contacts worldwide for investigations. Never work without private investigators. Contact The Private Group operations manager Chris Eastaughffe at pi@theprivategroup. com.au or phone 1300 966 103 in Australia.

You must prove the actual injuries such as depression with fMRI scans. Contact a neuroscience institute/hospital in your country and request fMRI scans *as well as* psychiatrists' and psychologists' written reports, which can interpret the scans for the court. Tremendous advances in neuroscience will prove the actual physical damage caused by depression and anxiety.

Once you have evidence that proves a workplace is dangerous *and* that injuries were the result of that particular workplace, then you can proceed.

The defense will maintain that the victim was weak and unable to cope in the workplace. *Au contraire*—according to research, victims are usually competent, successful, confidant, and qualified in contrast to bullies who are weak, jealous, and lack confidence (Rowell 2005). Bullies seek to weaken their victims by using one-on-one tactics to break the victim's spirit. Jealous co-workers could act collectively in mobbing activities as sycophants of the bully. The intent is to weaken or destroy the victim in this case, and conspiring to injure ventures into the criminal law arena (see the section on conspiracy). This is where you need the reports of professional private investigators that specialize in workplace issues.

Bullying is the term used in organizations, which makes it legitimate (Liefooghe et al 2010). Unlike bullying in schools, negative acts in organizations can be subtler. It is an abuse of formal power and is used as a strategy to influence and control employees (Hutchinson 2010). Human Resources worldwide resist admitting that there is bullying in their organizational culture. They fuss with bullying awareness programs to show that they are doing something. All these programs do is make the victim feel more powerless and lets the perpetrator get away with bullying.

This lawyers' guide describes the steps along the road to obtain compensation for your client. I liberally sprinkled this guide with case law so that when defense lawyers try to object to anything you say, you can clout them with authority from case law. I use Australian legislation; however, all democratic countries have similar laws relating to employment law. The references to the United Nations and the World Health Organization (WHO) apply to all member countries of the United Nations and WHO.

Medical Knowledge for Litigation

Events Chart

The Events Chart documents workplace events in logical order to demonstrate an emerging pattern of deviant behavior.

Date	Time	Event	Place	Witness	Action taken by you	Response to your action	Date of response	How did you fee/ react	Was the response adequate	Attach copy of relevant docs, e-mails, memos

Go through these patterns with your client, as sometimes what appears to be seemingly insignificant workplace behavior can be highly significant, especially if repeated on a regular basis.

Common law requires that information or an application containing a statement of offenses must at least condescend to identifying the essential factual ingredients of the actual offense (see *John L Pty Ltd v Attorney General (NSW)* (1987) 163 CLR 508). These facts need not be as extensive as those that a defendant might obtain on an application for particulars (see *De Romanis v Shbraa* (1977) NSWLR 264).

In *Johnson v Millar* (1937) 59 CLR 467, the court considered that information must specify the time, place, and manner of the defendant's acts or omissions and referred to the requirements being "fair information and reasonable particularity as to the nature of the offense charged."

Stress that it is in your client's best interest to take the chart seriously and complete it daily. If your client has been (or is being) injured from harassment/bullying, it's almost a foregone conclusion that the actions are happening on a daily basis. For harassment/bullying to be considered, it has to be continual and systematic, although, as we go to print, the unions in Australia are presently pushing for one single negative act to be considered bullying—much to the chagrin of the employers. However, we will deal with the law as it is now.

Meaning of "Event"

Events that happen in your client's workplace must not be:

A misconception of actual events
Considered to be irrational thinking

Workplace bullying/harassment can be insidious and the aim of the bully (and the defense lawyers) is to make your client appear to have *litigation neurosis* or *paranoid personality traits* or *irrational and emotional thinking*. One of these will be the main thrust of their argument.

Your client must complete the Events Chart daily, a difficult step because perpetrators of workplace bullying/harassment have the knack of producing an aura of *bon ami* and will throw their hands up in horror at the mere suggestion of being a bully. They will emphatically state that they were only *instigating new management strategies*. Your client will think that these events are inconsequential and will feel ashamed to be so affected by what appears as trivial incidents. Stress to your client that when every bullying action is recorded on the Events Chart a pattern will emerge. A bully designs these repetitive acts to intimidate and to make your client appear weak. Acts of bullying behavior are *events*.

In *Federal Broom Co. Pty Ltd v Semlitch* (1964) 110 CLR 626, Justice Windeyer stated that the contributing factor must be either *some event or occurrence in the course of the employment in which it was performed.*

Workplace bullying/harassment has caused serious biological injuries to your client, such as premonitory symptoms of fatigue, irritability, insomnia, and a feeling unable to cope. It is important to note that bullying/harassment has most likely affected your client's heart. That is why your client must undergo medical tests. Not only is this important for the sake of well being but it is important to have the injuries attributed to the workplace bullying/harassment.

It is an abrogation of human rights and indeed unlawful for your client to be deliberately injured in the workplace. When linking the events of workplace bullying to your client's injuries, you must prove that your client's nervous system was so affected that a physiological effect was induced. Be aware that lawyers for the defense will try to label this *emotional impulse*. There is no compensation for emotional impulse.

Aggravation, acceleration, exacerbation, or deterioration of a pre-existing condition are set out as conditions in the case of *Austin v Director-General of Education* (1994) 10 NSWCR 373.

Remember—an injury is neither a *frustration* nor an *emotional upset* as demonstrated in the case of *Thazine-Ayr v WorkCover* NSW (1995) 12 NSWCCR 304. No doubt the lawyers for the defense will repeat those words as a mantra, so be careful of those words.

Understanding the Beast

Bullying in the workplace is like terrorism in the workplace and has the same results. It is destructive, intimidating, and injurious and sometimes results in death. Bullying transcends age and sex. Bullies are usually in a position to get a mob of dull-witted sycophants to encourage the bully's destruction of the victim. Heinz Leymann (1990) labeled this behavior *mobbing.*

Victims dare not complain, fearing an unjustifiable punishment is dealt out by the system. Bullies are usually abusive and unpredictable and, in some cases, they goad their victims until they break. A university lecturer in Queensland jumped off the fifth floor of his department building to escape the bully who happened to be the dean of the faculty. Punishment dealt by bullies is usually unwarranted and unlawful; therefore, workplaces become unsafe. Bullying behavior is not just bad— it is deliberately destructive.

Einarsen (1998) stated that workplace bullying is either dispute-related arising from an initial or ongoing conflict; predatory, where a victim might be an unprovocative and opportunistic target, or a combination of these.

An employee who is bullied and victimized in the workplace has a legitimate grievance (Hall 1982). Workplace bullying is not merely an extreme form of social stressors. Bullying is prolonged frequent harassment behavior that is systematically aimed at a target person or group and is not the result of a difference of opinion in the workplace. It has three distinct dimensions that are intended to ostracize, marginalize, demean, intimidate, threaten, and injure the employee to the extent that a person doubts their self worth and their ability to function. Harassment/bullying techniques are characterized in three ways:

Non-verbal
Verbal
Workplace manipulation

Non-physical violent acts can create outcomes as serious as physical violence (Bowie 2002). Ongoing emotional, physical, verbal, and non-verbal abuse can negatively affect a person's sense of self as personally and professionally competent (Vickers 2010).

Victims of bullying/harassment doubt their sanity and doubt they will be believed. Note that the questions below do not result from social stressors in the work environment. Victims as targets are humiliated, denigrated, and aware of what is happening. These actions are deliberate ploys that empower bullies to dizzying heights of self-actualization.

Persons who are subjected to repeated negative acts in *all* parts of the workplace are considered bullied. Furthermore, victims of bullying must feel unable to defend themselves in these situations. Note that *all parts of the workplace include the obligatory workplace breakfast, conferences, and canteens—ALL places associated with the workplace.*

Ask your client the following questions, which indicate an issue of credibility in the workplace. Your client's response will become an important aspect of your case.

Have you experienced the following?

- Felt you have lost your credibility
- Felt you have failed to meet the expectations of others
- Felt embarrassed because of workplace bullying
- Felt you would lose the respect of someone important to you

- Felt uncomfortable
- Felt you were made to look silly
- Felt threatened.

This next set of questions will determine whether your client is being made to appear as a difficult person in the workplace. This will be evidenced when your client completes the Events Chart and will show the actions of the bully to be negative and continuous—thus complying with a clear definition of bullying.

Have you been made to believe the following?

- You are difficult to get on with
- You are unsupportive
- You are in the wrong
- You are intolerant
- You are incompetent

This set of questions will reveal if your client has a feeling of not being able to achieve success within the workplace.

- Are you being made to feel you are failing to meet your own expectations?
- Are you being made to feel you do not meet the expectations of the workplace?
- Do you feel hostility from others?

These three questions are to establish if your client has a feeling of no control in the workplace. Do you believe the following?

- A sense of injustice exists
- You have no control
- You are not getting enough support

At this stage, it is important to take your client through the Events Chart, which will become a logical documentation of events and responses to the harassment/bullying that your client is experiencing.

Unfortunately, most clients find completing the Events Chart on a regular basis extremely difficult—feeling as though they are reliving the events in the workplace. But you must insist on this as the workplace bullying activities have seriously impacted the health of your client. To gain an understanding of the seriousness of the injuries, I have included a summary of studies in this area to provide a deeper understanding of the serious impact workplace bullying has on physical health. Therefore, if bullying is allowed to exist in the workplace, then the workplace is a violent dangerous place that inflicts injuries—usually with the knowledge of management. This puts management (and the bullies) fairly in the firing line for allowing the workplace to become a dangerous place. That is against the law in all democratic countries and any injuries as a result of allowable bullying by management are compensable.

It was Zegans (1982) who formulated the means by which stress impacts health by the responses of the physiological functioning. Bullying leads to burnout and the studies of Lubinski (1994) and Maslach (1982) found that the work environment could produce an insidious and vicious physical and psychological toll on an individual.

In a study financed by the World Health Organization (WHO), Von Korff and Simon (1996) analyzed the relationship between pain and depression. When chronic pain and depression co-occur, physical and psychological illnesses become enmeshed in ways that challenge conventional notions of the boundaries between physical disease and psychological disorder. Their epidemiological study determined a trait of susceptibility to both dysphoric physical symptoms (including pain) and psychological symptoms (including depression) and a state of somatosensory amplification in which psychological distress amplifies dysphoric physical sensations. Von Korff and Simon in this WHO collaborative project on Psychological Problems in General Health Care synthesized the correlation between psychological illness and chronic pain. At the end of this manual is a template for your brief to the doctors and psychiatrists. They should elaborate on this subject in their reports and add the appropriate medical terminology.

Bullying is about power and power equates to entitlement. According to Goodwin et al (2000), a power holder feels entitled to judge others, which increases the power holder's confidence in their own beliefs. A perception in Western culture is that those who have the necessary skills earn power and therefore their power is valid.

Bullies share the following characteristics:

- Desire power
- Find power exhilarating and reinforcing
- Desire to harm the victim
- Derive pleasure when exerting power over the victim
- Exhibit systematic and repetitive behavior
- Display psychosocial deviant behavior in the workplace and multiple behavioral patterns
- Use power to destroy—either a person or a person's confidence

Workplace bullies usually single out victims within the work relationship. Often the bully takes pleasure in seeing a victim's fear, which validates the bully's power. This is then reinforced by the silent overwhelming approval of the audience within the workplace. The silent approval is akin to thunderous applause for award-winning bullying, which, of course, would call for an encore and encourage the bullying to continue.

Bullying is not a legitimate management tool but rather a means to destroy and injure—clearly a breach of all workplace health and safety legislation in democratic countries worldwide. Bullying becomes a stressful situation that commences a chain reaction and is far more than misconduct. It is a form of employment discrimination that consists of offensive, abusive, or threatening behavior directed at a person or group.

The bullies and their defense lawyers will no doubt use the perennial defenses: it was only interpersonal conflict, not bullying; it was only a legitimate comment; or I was just giving advice. The usual tactic is to fault the victim.

Bullies believe they have earned their power and that it is valid. They believe that a strong leader/individual has control and should show it. As the bully's self evaluation inflates, the victim's evaluation deteriorates.

Tactics used by bullies to cement their power and prove they are in control include:

- Sabotaging work and equipment
- Sending memos containing inaccurate accusations and information
- Interfering with correspondence
- Giving menial tasks to humiliate a person
- Maliciously over monitoring
- Making constant changes to confuse and make a person look stupid
- Supplying inaccurate information
- Setting a person up to fail
- Blocking applications for training
- Changing personal reports or appraisals
- Bullying a person into signing an incorrect performance appraisal
- Destroying peer relationships behind a person's back

Cluster bullying is detrimental to health, undermines confidence, and removes human dignity. Incidences of this type of bullying must be recorded on the Events Chart.

Interviews with many victims revealed the following reactions to bullying/harassment in the workplace.

- Pretending to be ill
- Feeling nauseated in the morning (vomiting at the thought of more bullying)

- Fantasizing about ways to kill the bully
- Experiencing Insomnia
- Feeling as though the person is being repeatedly punched in the stomach
- Feeling isolated (not being believed and being made out to be a liar and troublemaker)
- Being picked on because of careless mistakes
- Doubting self worth
- Feeling an inability to cope
- Experiencing a feeling of going mad or crazy

Persistent bullying is detrimental to well being, health, and causes serious workplace injuries. In some cases, a person attempts suicide as a means of escaping the bullying (see the horror cases at the end of this book).

Symbolic violence was first termed by the French sociologist of culture Pierre Bourdieu (1979) who developed the context of psychosocial workplace behavior. He believed that dominant classes or class factions impose ruling ideologies upon dominated groups by legitimizing their interests and beliefs as natural and right, whereby the subjugation of employees implicitly defended the stratified order of the institution. This stratified order was then perceived as the natural order of domination. As a result of legitimizing psychosocial workplace behavior, bullied employees suffer from anxiety and depression.

It was held in *Baltic Shipping Co v Dillon* (1992-1993) 176 CLR 344 that employees must be able to work quietly and free from molestation or vexation.

When interviewing your client, it is important to note the full extent of employment. Employment does not merely mean the act of being employed, but the work that the worker is required to do (see *Stewart v NSW Police Service* (1998) 17 NSWCCR 202). In *Thom v Sinclair,* (1917) AC 127, Lord Shaw of Dumferline stated that employment included all its elements, "its nature, its conditions, its obligations and its incidents"—which would include the obligatory workplace events: breakfast, conferences, trips, recreation, the Christmas party, and so on. Use this case to include *every* aspect of the workplace.

According to Lord Dunedin in *Charles R Davidson & Co v Mc Robb,* (1918) AC 304, the term employment naturally extends to matters "naturally incidental" to the contract. Also note this particular case if the bullying occurs outside the workplace but in a work environment. Do not allow the defense lawyers to state that if certain incidents occurred outside the actual workplace they are not considered events in the workplace.

Kitto J. in *Federal Broom Co Pty Ltd v Semlitch* (1964) 110 CLR 626 held that "employment" refers to *some incident or state of affairs to which the worker was exposed in the performance of his duties and to which he would not otherwise have been exposed.* In this case, Windeyer J. held that employment included "some characteristic of the work or the conditions in which it was performed . . . (and) . . . the contributing factor must, in my opinion, be either some event or occurrence in the course of the employment or some characteristic of the work performed or the conditions in which it was performed." The characteristic of employment must also include that which a worker was reasonably required, expected, or authorized to do to carry out the work.

In the case of *Humphrey Earl Ltd v Speechley* (1951) 84 CLR 126, Dixon J. defined the peripheral of employment as *The acts of a workman, which form part of his service to his employer, are done, needless to say, in the course of his employment. The service is not confined to the actual performance of the work, which the workman is employed to do. Whatever is incidental to the performance of the work is covered by the course of employment.*

This, of course, would include any activity connected with work—remember breakfasts, conferences, and workshops are usually outside the actual place of work. These are "incidental to the performance of work" so make sure your client is aware that all bullying events that are connected with work are documented on the Events Chart.

Toxic Workplace Behavior

Workplace bullying/harassment causes injuries, which are like malignant cancers. Unlike a cyst, cancer does not have defined edges, as the cancer boundaries are indefinable. Bullying/harassment in the workplace is like a cancer—fuzzy edges that can spread into all places.

Workplace behavior penetrates like a cancerous cell: the destruction has begun but the symptoms are not apparent. Have your client determine if any of these events occurred in the workplace and, if so, write the questions on the Events Chart.

- Have malicious, unfounded, and groundless rumors been spread in order to undermine your credibility?
- Have you been persistently criticized either privately or within the hearing of others? What was said?
- Has a colleague or supervisor delighted in persecution through instilling fear and issuing threats either to your face or through a third party?
- Have you been repeatedly shouted at and sworn at both publicly and in private?
- Have you been subjected to personal insults or name calling in public or private?
- Are you labeled at work?
- Does you boss/supervisor fly into rages usually over some trivial matter to instill fear in you?
- Does your boss/supervisor or a work colleague publicly humiliate you?
- Are you constantly criticized?

- Do you feel you are secluded or ignored and excluded?
- Are your efforts constantly undervalued?
- Does your supervisor or colleague get the praise and kudos for your ideas and work?
- Have you been manipulated into a smaller office in a corner?
- Does your boss/colleague deliberately talk to a third party and obviously isolate you?
- Does your boss/supervisor dispense punishment out of the blue usually for something you cannot remember?
- Are you given tasks that are not suitable to your physical capabilities or health?
- Have you been threatened with a physical attack?
- Have you suffered from a physical attack?
- Is your work sabotaged?
- Has someone tampered with your computer or equipment?
- Do you receive long memos, which contain inaccurate accusations and inaccurate information?
- Has someone interfered with your mail or e-mail?
- Are you given menial tasks or has your area of responsibility been vastly diminished?
- Are you being maliciously over monitored with or without your knowledge?
- Have you been supplied with incorrect information?
- Is information deliberately being withheld from you?
- Do you receive constant changes over guidelines and targets?
- Have you been set up to fail?
- Are your promotion applications blocked? (Strictly speaking, this is not a bullying act but it would have to be linked to other actions and circumstances.)
- Have your personal reports and appraisals been changed?

- Were you bullied or harassed into signing an incorrect performance appraisal?
- Have your relationships with your peers been destroyed behind your back?

Socio-deviant behaviors are not isolated incidents and are usually cumulative and clustered to produce devastating effects on employees who are targeted because they are in a subordinate position.

Psychiatry in Court

Question your client to establish that there is a post-traumatic stress disorder (PTSD). These classifications of symptoms were developed by Scrignar (1997) and are accepted in court. Although the following list will provide an overall picture, you must get an expert psychiatrist's report.

Nervousness

Is your client apprehensive, on edge, tense, jumpy, easily startled, and fearful?

Preoccupation with the trauma

Does your client talk a great deal about the events, even at home?

Pain or physical discomfort

Does your client complain of pain or physical discomfort that appears disproportionate to the actual injury?

Sleeplessness

Is your client suffering from insomnia with resultant tiredness and fatigue?

Flashbacks and nightmares

Does your client relive the trauma during flashbacks or nightmares with similar emotional reactions as if the events were happening again? (This is very common with victims of workplace bullying/harassment).

Deterioration of performance

Does your client experience inability or difficulty in performing usual activities: work and family responsibilities, social and recreational activities, or any activity engaged in before the bullying/harassment events?

Phobia

Does your client experience fearfulness and avoidance of the place where the events occurred or extreme apprehension associated with some activity related to the bullying/harassment events?

Personality change

Has your client become withdrawn, moody, irritable, distracted, forgettable, and unlike his/her usual self?

Dudgeon

Has your client demonstrated a retributive attitude and frequent unprovoked outbursts of anger with complaints about the carelessness of others?

Depression

Has your client lost self-confidence and shown a pessimistic attitude, coupled with brooding about past events and a feeling of self-pity?

Psychiatrist v Psychiatrist

You will be sending your client to a psychiatrist and, of course, the lawyers for the defense will insist upon your client seeing *their* psychiatrist. Each professional will give a test from which they are required to write a report. The psychiatrist for the defense lawyer will try to portray your client as a liar or try to show that the condition pre-existed. Most victims of prolonged workplace bullying/harassment suffer from post-traumatic stress disorder (PTSD) that can last a lifetime or linger for years.

Go over the questions that psychiatrists will ask because victims of workplace bullying/harassment are so traumatized that they might leave out vital information believing that it is not important. Psychiatrists use a book called *The Diagnostic and Statistical Manual DSM-4*. The diagnostic criteria for PTSD are shown on page 427.

The following questions are asked by a psychiatrist to establish post-traumatic stress disorder:

Have you experienced an event/events at work that involved your serious injury?

A policeman experienced multiple negative events: his prayer was ripped off his computer, he was laughed at when he showed he was upset at the death of his dog, and he was ridiculed by peers when he, a non drinker, refused to go to the pub for "bonding". These seemingly small incidents are considered as cluster bullying. Incidentally, that policeman got over $300,000 as an out-of-court settlement, and the case was closely watched by the police commissioner. The State Government was horrified that an avalanche of claims could have occurred if this scenario and the circumstances became public.

Has your response involved fear or helplessness?

Make sure your client documents everything on the Events Chart including medications, which must be disclosed. Make sure your client discloses all incidents that are connected with workplace bullying/harassment. A senior accountant from a national large firm (one of the "Big 6" in Australia) told me she vomited when she got to work each day because she feared what the day would bring. She was quite senior and very clever, but she was the victim of office jealousy, manipulation, humiliation, and bullying. A former serviceman told me he still has nightmares—even though it has now been twenty years since he left the services.

Are your recollections recurrent?

Yes—of course they are. Recollections of workplace bullying/harassment are like an old cracked record. Your client will suffer from insomnia, depression, and then anger, making it difficult for your client to focus on anything else that is happening outside the work environment. Families suffer as the bullying/harassment starts to affect family life.

Do you constantly dream of the events (incidents in the workplace)?

Undoubtedly—your client will wake up in a sweat as a result of these experiences. These dreams, which are akin to childhood nightmares, are very real and threatening. Make sure your client documents these dreams, in detail, and their repetitiveness.

Do you relive your workplace experiences in flashbacks?

Of course your client does. When I was doing radio talk back programs, the number of people who relived the workplace experiences for decades astounded me. This indicates long-term injuries that your client has sustained from an unsafe workplace.

Do you suffer psychological distress in your work situation?

Every victim of workplace bullying/harassment feels distress. Make sure your client documents everything on the Events Chart to demonstrate a clear pattern of how the workplace made your client ill and injured.

How do you react physically to your work environment?

Make sure your client lists every action of bullying—no matter how insignificant. Be sure to explain to your client that bullies pride themselves of being clever and that they set out to make sure their victim is perceived as paranoid. That is why you will need a pattern of documented actions and words that would constitute repeated bullying. Your client must describe all physical symptoms resulting from bullying/harassment— migraines, headaches, stomach problems, bowel problems, lower back pain, nausea, depression, and anxiety.

All of these points must be detailed so that your client's post-traumatic stress disorder from the workplace bullying/harassment will not be diagnosed as *mild depression*. Psychiatrists for the defense will endeavor to prove *mild depression* in order to trivialize your client's claim for damages due to workplace injuries. Reassure your client that victims who suffer from bullying/harassment can feel angry for years because the perpetrators are *getting away with it.*

Medical Reports

Before you send your client for a medical examination, make sure your client clearly understands what is required.

Report the client's previous health status:

Stress to your client the importance of not omitting anything. Lawyers for the defense will easily uncover omissions or inaccuracies, which could show your client to be unreliable. Make the doctor aware of how your client's health has suffered due to other factors, so that the doctor's report is credible. If your client's workplace situation has exacerbated the person's health status, all factors should be taken into account.

How has the situation impacted upon your client's life, family, and health? Your client should explain how the workplace situation has affected his/her life and the ability to work. Your client may need to be retrained or paid to do further study. A young policeman who was bullied needed to study for a new career at Bond University ($100,000) plus accommodation plus private tuition (as he had been so traumatized) plus books and materials plus living expenses plus ongoing psychiatric counseling—plus plus plus! Your client's deteriorated health has also impacted upon his/her family so you must also detail the dislocation of the family that has arisen due to health problems from bullying/harassment in the workplace.

How has the work situation changed your client's health and family life?

Have your client list changing circumstances of family life including events and consequences on the Events Chart. Explain that the doctor's diagnosis should link your client's physical deterioration to a meaningful explanation that is related to your client's workplace injuries and show how physical symptoms have changed.

The doctor's report should comprehensive:

- Document changes in any of the symptoms
- Contain such terminology as functional disability and clinical impairment
- Scientifically explain your client's medical problems
- Describe the examinations and the tests used and include the reasons for ordering them
- Include a speculation, in the doctor's opinion, about the basis of your client's clinical profile
- Stress that the doctor is not there to merely proscribe Prozac or other antidepressants but to understand the underlying causes for prescribing such medicine and to relate it to workplace events.

Injuries Resulting from Bullying

By the time your client walks into your office, feeling nervous and humiliated at being unable to cope with the workplace situation, the person has probably been self-medicating for some time. It is helpful to say you understand the injuries suffered and the reason for them. You will get appreciative nods as they relate the workplace events. Nine times out of ten, your client will be suffering from many injuries. Go through the following list of injuries to assist your client in completing the Events Chart.

Heart palpitations

This is a symptom of extreme stress, due to fearfulness as a result of your client's workplace situation
    Skin irritation and blotches
    Symptoms are often associated with nerves due to the abuse and humiliation suffered by your client. Have your client list all medications presently being prescribed for skin problems.

Insomnia

This is a common problem brought about by anxiety due to persistent bullying.

Anxiety

Anxiety is usually associated with the unpredictability of your client's work environment as well as the humiliation and fear it induces. This must *never* be trivialized as an emotional disorder. Be aware that lawyers for the defense will use the term "emotional disorder" like a mantra. Object immediately as this term will jeopardize and trivialize your client's claim. Lawyers for the defense are not psychologists or psychiatrists so their evaluation of your client's injuries is unsubstantiated. Carefully go through the anxiety section in this manual and familiarize yourself with what anxiety really means to justify your objection to the judge.

Backache

Tension and feelings of anxiety produce severe pain in the lower back and the neck. Have your client record the repetitiveness of backaches and make sure your client's psychotherapist is aware that the backaches are caused by your client's workplace situation.

Stomach and bowel problems

Symptoms are the result of nerves and stress-related problems that are caused by the unpredictable nature of the workplace bullying/harassment.

Lethargy

Usually associated with depression, lethargy can develop when a victim of workplace bullying/harassment is constantly undermined and no longer feels that anything accomplished is of any value.

Feelings of nausea

Usually nausea occurs at the very thought of the workplace situation. It is associated with sweating and shaking and most likely happens when the bullying/harassment is disguised with honeyed tones that belie the true meaning of what is being said.

Migraines or severe headaches

These can occur on a regular basis when persistent bullying/ harassment is present in the workplace.

Severe depression

Almost bordering on thoughts of suicide, depression can be brought on by a sense of injustice and powerlessness with no end in sight. A few years ago a university lecturer reacting to repeated bullying from the head of the faculty, jumped from a fifth floor window of a university building. Recently, several suicides have occurred in the armed services, which have been attributed to bullying/harassment.

Murderous feelings and acute anger

These feeling are brought on by continuous bickering and undermining. A few years ago, a victim of bullying snapped and killed the supervisor of a courier company in Sydney.

Panic attacks

Frustration and anxiety occur when your client has suffered persistent bullying/harassment.

Constant feelings of irritability

These are stress related due to an inability to cope with the workplace situation and the additional anxiety suffered by your client.

No motivation

The consistent bullying/harassment has led your client to the stage where he asks himself, "Why bother?"

Loss of self-confidence and self-esteem

Your client's self worth and self-confidence has eroded, making your client unable to stand up to the bully or to seek other employment.

Tell your client to take the following steps to move closer to dealing with the situation:

- Go to specialists only who are experienced in dealing with workplace bullying/harassment. You will know who these doctors are in your area.
- Go to a psychiatrist and psychologist—assist your client here. At the end of this manual, there is a template for writing a brief to a psychiatrist/psychologist. Do not assume that doctors and psychiatrists are psychic. The template details what you need.
- Keep a record of incidents based on the Events Chart. Your client will tell you that it is too much trouble to maintain; however, you must emphasize that without it—there is no case.

Prior Injuries

Even if your client has suffered a prior injury and is further injured at work, that "sudden or identifiable change" can be classified as a personal injury. If lawyers for the defense try to suggest that your client's injuries are a result of something that happened in the past, go straight to *Kennedy Cleaning Services Pty Ltd v Petklosa* (2000) 74 ALR 626. If your client has a sudden change to an existing condition, then the workplace is liable if conditions in the workplace cause the sudden change to your client's injuries. The following case shows how courts deal with prior injuries.

In *Kennedy Cleaning Services Pty Ltd v Petkosa*, Mrs. Petkoska, who was employed by the Kennedy Cleaning Company, suffered a stroke. Prior to this, she had been diagnosed as suffering from rheumatic mitral valve disease, a heart condition that, in some cases, manifests itself with bouts of quivering (fibrillation) that may lead to the release of a clot (embolism) into the blood stream. Medical opinions unanimously determined that her employment was not a contributing factor to the contraction of the underlying mitral stenosis in her heart. However, the Full Federal Court did not relieve Kennedy Cleaning from liability.

Circumstances that aggravate a disease, injury, or medical condition must be shown to be work related. It doesn't matter if the original disease or injury was work related just so long as work aggravates your client's present condition. Depending on the circumstances, your client's doctor should make the workplace the major or significant factor in the injuries suffered.

This is to comply with the workplace legislation of your state or territory.

In *Zickar v MGH Plastics Industries Pty Ltd* (1996) 187 CLR 310, it was recognized that an injury, being of a sudden or identifiable physiological change, could qualify with the ordinary application that appears in workers compensation legislation even if the change was internal to the body of the worker. Therefore, those changes in your client's body do not have to be external or necessarily have been produced by external causes.

The sections on depression and anxiety below provide medical details associated with the internal injuries.

If you can establish that your client had a sudden and ascertainable or dramatic physiological change or disturbance of the normal physiological state, then that should qualify for the characterization of an *injury.*

The workplace bullying/harassment that your client has endured has produced internal injuries. If these injuries occurred during employment, then these physiological changes and changes to your client's normal state can be attributed to *workplace injuries.*

Lawyers for the defense will argue that your client's injuries were caused by other reasons, act as though your client has no case, and even lie about the prospects of your client's case. Have your client document the events causing injuries even if the injuries are internal. This will keep the defendant from escaping liability.

Your client's record of injuries must be linked to certain conditions:

- The deliberate behavior was meant to inflict harm
- Top management knew the behavior would inflict harm
- Top management failed to do anything—this is important

- Top management could foresee that such behavior would inflict harm
- Bullying/harassment endured by your client has produced internal injuries during the course of employment. These physiological changes that happen during the course of employment constitute an injury.

Remember—you must establish that your client:

Suffered a sudden or dramatic physiological change
Suffered a disturbance of the client's normal physiological state
Suffered injury within the protected period of employment

Once you establish these criteria, the injury qualifies as compensable. Workplace bullying/harassment does produce internal injuries and the physiological changes to your client's normal state will be an *injury* if it happens in a workplace environment.

It is prudent for an employee to establish that the workplace injuries received would have had the same effect upon another person under the same conditions. In *Vozza v Tooth & Co Limited* (1964) 112 CLR 316, Windeyer J. (with the concurrence of Mc Tieman, Kitto, Taylor and Owen J. J.) stated that it must be established by evidence that the employer: *Unreasonably failed to take measures and adopt means, reasonably open to him in all the circumstances, which would have protected the plaintiff from the dangers of his task without unduly impeding its accomplishment.*

However, where the employer has knowledge or at least the means of knowledge of a particular susceptibility to injury in the employee, then that will affect the steps, which must be taken in order to comply with the obligation to take reasonable care.

The Sensitive Personality

Lawyers for the defense will try to denigrate your client if your client is a sensitive person. Chief Justice Barwick in the case of *Mt Isa Mines Limited v Pusey* (1971) 125 CLR 383 stated: *The idea of a man of normal emotional fiber, as distinct from a man sensitive, susceptible and more easily disturbed emotionally and mentally is I think imprecise and scientifically inexact . . . I am not convinced that the defendant . . . can escape liability by showing that, unknown to him, a person who suffered harm was easily harmed.*

Even if your client is a sensitive person and has an "eggshell personality", note that the English case of *Brice v Brown* (1984) 1 All ER 997 stated that full damages were payable no matter how serious the condition may be, because the plaintiff's case was genuine.

These are tactics of defense lawyers. Be aware that the defense will use all of these:

- Try to show that your client had a misperception of actual events
- Say that your client's thinking was irrational
- Say that your client rationalized past innocuous events that led to the client's illness

Link the workplace bullying/harassment as the significant contributing factor to your client's injuries. Stress again the importance of the Events Chart to your client.

You must make sure your client does not appear as merely distressed from an emotional impulse—explain to your client that there is no compensation for being distressed and emotional.

In *Bahatia v State Rail Authority* (NSW) (1997) 14 NSWCCR 568, Justice Burke said that a post-traumatic stress disorder is a physiological injury but an emotional impulse is not. Watch for any suggestion of emotional impulse or words to that effect that will be used by the defense lawyers. Keep to terms like *post-traumatic stress disorder, anxiety, depression,* and *physical injuries.*

Depression

Depression, a serious condition that must not be trivialized, is one of the most common injuries that your client will suffer as a victim of workplace bullying/harassment.

Depression will cause the following changes in a person:

- Reduced gray matter density in the left temporal cortex, which includes the hippocampus in chronic depression
- An increased perfusion in cingulated and paralimbic areas
- A reduction in altanserin uptake in the right hemisphere, which also includes posterolateral, orbitofrontal and the anterior insular cortex

A brain scan at a neuroscience department at a hospital or institute will provide the evidence of depression and what it is doing to your client biologically. When requesting medical reports, make sure the doctor/psychiatrist actually lists these injuries. Otherwise, there is a tendency for the word "depression" to be trivialized as a "state of mind." Be careful of that. Depression is certainly not a *mental condition.* It is a very real physical injury. Therefore, if your client's workplace is causing your client's depression, the workplace is unsafe because your client has been injured. Depression has intrinsic biological disadvantages and most signs of a neurological examination in adult psychiatry can be reliably evaluate and validate against techniques such as the EEG, which is an electroencephalography that registers the electrical potentials recorded by the electroencephalograph.

Insist that your client have an EEG so that your client's injuries are evaluated and validated. To validate that the injuries are substantially linked to the events of the workplace, you must stress to your client to keep up the Events Chart. I have repeated this because clients often find it too hard to go over the events every night and write them up. They will stop doing this if you don't keep nagging them.

Physical signs of depression cannot be underestimated. Canberra psychiatrist, Dr. Ramish Gupta (2002) has stated that the physical signs of depression have their importance in differential diagnosis and as a qualitative care issue. Furthermore, these have serious clinical and medico-legal ramifications providing the objective evidence of subjective complaints. Depression is a physical injury that can be proved by advances in structural biology, genetic engineering, and brain imaging.

To assist your case, I have included the Stouthard's Netherlands study on depression that measured weights for fifty-three diseases of public health importance. Each disease was defined in terms associated with the average levels of disability, handicap, mental well being, pain, and cognitive impairment. On a scale of 0.00 to 1.00, moderate depression was 0.30 to 0.40 and severe depression was on a par with moderate brain injury at 0.65 to 0.80. This gives you an excellent focus on the depression levels suffered by your client. Make sure you have your client's psychiatrist validate the Stouthard's Netherlands study for your client's medical evaluation.

Stouthard's *Disability Weights for Diseases* (2000)
Department of Public Health, Netherlands

WEIGHT	DISEASE, STAGE, SEVERITY LEVEL OR SEQUELA
0.00-0.01	Gingivitis, dental caries.
0.01-0.05	Mild asthma, mild vision loss, mild hearing loss, basal cancer cell skin.
0.05-0.1	Low back pain, uncomplicated diabetes case, mild stable angina (NYHA 1-2).
0.10-0.15	Mild depression, osteoarthritis (radiological grade 2) of hip or knee, epilepsy.
0.15-0.20	Mild/moderate panic disorder, spin bifida (sacral), HIV seropositive.
0.20-0.30	Non-invasive breast cancer or tumour < 2 cm (diagnostic/treatment phase).
0.30-0.40	Moderate depression, multiple sclerosis in relapsing-remitting phase, severe asthma, chronic hepatitis B infection with active viral replication, deafness.
0.40-0.50	Severe vision loss, medium-level spinabifida (L3-L5), osteoarthritis (grade 3-4), small operable small cell lung cancer, moderate intellectual disability (IQ 35-49).
0.50-0.65	Paraplegia, AIDS (first stage), chronic bronchitis or emphysema.

WEIGHT	DISEASE, STAGE, SEVERITY LEVEL OR SEQUELA
0.65-0.80	Disseminated breast cancer, severe depression, moderately severe brain injury resulting in permanent impairments, extreme intellectual disability (IQ < 20).
0.80-1.00	Severe schizophrenia, disseminated colorectal cancer, severe dementia, alcoholic psychosis, quadriplegia, stroke with multiple permanent impairments, end-stage Parkinson's disease.

In relating your client's depression to Stouthard's Netherlands study, the psychiatrist will clarify the extent of damage to your client's health and put it into perspective. When you link your client's depression to the workplace situation, the seriousness of the injury is apparent.

The Stouthard study used specific disease stages or severity levels so that judgments were not required on the distribution of disease stage in terms of the associated average levels of disability, handicap, mental well being, pain, and cognitive impairment using a modified version of the EuroQol health status instrument. Therefore, if your client is diagnosed as suffering from severe depression as a result of workplace bullying/ harassment, then it is extremely serious.

Endogenous depression is also known as a major or biological depression, which causes an imbalance in the body's chemistry. Remember, depression is an actual physical disability and not a state of mind. Depression must never be termed as "pure psychiatric." Make sure your client's doctor details the chemical imbalance so there is neither misconception nor misunderstanding as to the true extent of your client's workplace injuries. Note these important points for your case:

- Your client's depression is a result of workplace bullying/harassment
- Your client has a physical injury that occurred due to the unsafe workplace
- Management permitted bullying to occur, which made the workplace unsafe
- Management was aware of the bullying
- Management foresaw that workplace bullying was injuring your client's health and safety

Stress and depression due to workplace bullying/harassment has caused your client a biological injury. Under no circumstances should you allow the lawyers for the defense to insist that your client's depression is *merely psychological*.

To enrage the lawyers for the defense when they try to claim that your client's depression is all in your client's mind, quote O'Keene's (2000) *Evolving model of depression as an expression of multiple interacting factors*. Have your client's psychiatrist validate that this applies to your client.

O'Keene identified different stressors which activate selective stress responses in the body. The most commonly activated of these systems is the hypothalamic pituitary adrenal (HPA) axis. There is activation of the HPA axis following psychological stress, which, according to Keene, involves the stress neurotransmitters 5-hydroxytryptamine (5-HT) or noradrenaline (NA). Stimulation of either of these neurotransmitter systems results in CHR (corticotropin-releasing hormone) release from the hypothalamus and subsequent release of adrenocorticotrophic hormone (ACTH) from the anterior pituitary gland. The word "stress" now takes on a whole new dimension. This means that stress and depression have caused your client an actual biological injury. This terminology will dispel any suggestion from the defense lawyers that *it is all in the mind.*

Remember—the aim of the defense lawyers is to trivialize your client's injuries and have the person appear as over emotional or someone who will either expand on the truth or not get the truth right.

The defense lawyers will set out to have your client admit the following:

- The so-called bullying was the person's perception— it really didn't happen
- The person is sensitive
- The person is experiencing a period of emotional distress
- No one else complained
- The defense lawyers will try to plant the seed of self-doubt and self-worth in your client. Get your client ready for this.

Anxiety

Like the word "depression," the word "anxiety" has the connotation of having a stressed state of mind, although it is actually a serious physical condition. A person suffering from anxiety has hypoglycaemia or low blood glucose that interferes with the function of the brain.

Anxiety causes problems in the abdominal organs. The sympathetic nervous system is one of the automatic regulatory systems, which oversees the processes of the body. Most organs have sympathetic and parasympathetic fibers. These oppose each other but their interaction controls the functions of the many organ systems in the body. Prolonged anxiety disrupts this happy equilibrium and spasms will occur in the hollow organs such as the large bowel and the bladder as well as dyspepsia from disordered contractions in the stomach.

Medical tests for the physical symptoms of anxiety will show that your client has experienced the following:

- Changes in blood flow causing shut down of blood flow through the skin. Diverted blood flow and subsequent sweating makes hands cold and clammy
- Changes in the activity of the internal organs
- Spasms in the lower esophagus
- Tension headaches
- Chronic headaches
- Stiff and sore muscles particularly in the neck and upper shoulders

- Increased tension of both agonist and antagonist muscle groups causing tremors and shakes, most likely seen in the hands
- Backaches and pains in the chest because the chest muscles cannot rest easily
- Increased rapid heart rate resulting in flutters and palpitations due to occasional irregular heartbeats. These abnormal beats are a consequence of the increased irritability of the heart caused by activation of the sympathetic nervous system fibers.

When your client suffers from anxiety, the body is put on alert as the flow of blood is diverted from non-essential functions so that the nerve network is stimulated. The network, known as the parasympathetic nervous system, activates when the body is resting. However, with frequent anxiety reactions, the parasympathetic nervous system must oppose the effects of adrenaline and noradrenaline that are released during anxiety. As a result of this, there can be irregular contractions in the hollow organs in the body.

If workplace bullying/harassment is resulting in anxiety, you can see how this will produce serious physical consequences. It is important that you do not allow anxiety to be trivialized by the defense lawyers. There is also a tendency for the judge to see anxiety as a state of mind—so make sure you are armed with detailed doctors' reports. You want to stress that the physical injury was caused by an unsafe workplace that permits bullying/harassment.

At this stage, be aware that the lawyers for the defense will try to introduce words such as *frustration* and *emotional upsets*. These words do not constitute an injury. Keep using the words *injury, impairment,* and *disability* and make the workplace the major contributing and substantial factor to your client's injuries. Stress that your client's nervous system was so affected by the

41

workplace bullying/harassment that physiological effects were induced. Prove this with fMRI scans.

If your client suffers from anxiety based on other issues, the anxiety caused by the workplace bullying/harassment must not aggravate, accelerate, exacerbate, or deteriorate your client's previous condition. But of course, it will! Have another look at the case of Kennedy in the section on Prior Injuries. Any aggravation of an existing injury has to be linked to the workplace bullying/harassment. The doctor's report should state that the workplace was a *substantial* cause of the injury. Make sure the doctor's reports use terminology that is in the workplace legislation of your state or territory. A template for briefing a doctor in these cases is provided at the end of this manual.

Disease

In *Comcare v Moori* (1996) 132 ALR 690, it was held that only conditions involving a disturbance of the normal functions of the body and mind fall within the term "disease" and therefore are defined as injuries under the *Safety Rehabilitation and Compensation Act* (Cth) 1988 (the Act). Your jurisdiction will have similar legislation.

Disease is defined in section 4 to mean any ailment or aggravation of such an ailment suffered by an employee, being an ailment or aggravation that was contributed to in a material degree by the employee's employment.

Ailment (s4) means any physical or mental ailment, disorder, defect, or morbid condition (whether sudden or gradual).

Injury is defined by s4 (the Act) as a disease suffered by an employee of a physical or mental injury (other than a disease) or an aggravation of a physical or mental injury (other than a disease) arising out of, or in the course of, the employee's employment.

It is important to note that a disease, injury, or aggravation suffered must not be as a result of failure by an employee to obtain a promotion or benefit in connection with the person's employment. Therefore, it is important in your statement that the injuries suffered were not from a lack of promotion or lack of work benefits.

In *Comcare v Moori,* the disturbance of the normal functions of body and mind are within the term "disease" and that is an injury.

Have your client disclose all other life issues that could cause an injury. Reassure your client that a previous condition doesn't matter as long as the workplace bullying/harassment is aggravating the previous condition. Ensure that the workplace bullying/harassment is significant, substantial, and the major factor contributing to your client's injuries. You will need to identify the exact wording in the workplace legislation of your state or territory. All democratic countries will basically have the same conditions for workplace health and safety. Quote exactly from the applicable legislation in your jurisdiction and use cases to support your argument.

Impairment

The ordinary meaning of the word "impair", from which the word "impairment" is derived, is

". . . to damage or weaken something, especially in terms of its quality or strength . . . " (Chambers 2004).

Taber's *Cyclopedic Medical Dictionary* (2004) defines it as "any loss or abnormality of psychological, physiological, or anatomical structure or function." In formulating the *Guides to the Evaluation of Permanent Impairment* (2001), the American Medical Association has adopted this meaning of "impairment" as *a loss of use or derangement of any body part or organ system or organ function.*

These meanings have in common an element of loss or abnormality in a body part or system or an element of loss or partial loss of the function of a body part or system with regard to what is normal. It is to your client's advantage that the doctors' reports are liberally sprinkled with the word "impairment" when assessing the injuries sustained by your client due to workplace bullying/harassment.

Bullying Can Cause a Heart Condition

Your client's suffering from the workplace situation does induce identifiable physiological changes such as an increase in the pulse rate and an increase in blood pressure, which puts pressure on the heart. Anxiety produces a rapid heart rate, and your client may experience flutters and palpitations because of the irregular heartbeats. This occurs because of increased irritability of the heart, which is caused by the activation of the sympathetic nervous system fibers. The stimulus of the sympathetic nervous system (the part of the body that prepares for flight or fight) involves the secretion of a rush of adrenaline, which is prone to precipitate the dreaded arrhythmias, which often result in angina and subsequent cardiac arrest.

Studies at St. Vincent's Hospital in Sydney, by former visiting cardiologist Dr. John Raftos, have shown that coronary subjects who have problems with anxiety, depression, or psycho-social problems due to work have an increased incidence of heart disease symptoms and angina in particular. Workplace bullying/harassment puts a dynamic load on the heart that could result in cardiac arrest or myocardial infarction. For example—a worker that is being abused by a boss and is not in a position to hit back, drops dead after the event. The stress on the heart may not be apparent for some hours; however, angina can also occur during the REM (Rapid Eye Movement) sleep. Any ischemic changes occur on an electro-cardiogram. If there is an acute ischemic change during the night, death could occur.

According to Dr Raftos, *acute emotional stress can result in identifiable physiological changes, increases in pulse rates and blood pressure and these, depending upon the stimulus and upon the recipient, may be absolutely maximal. This could be the hardest work the heart does.*

Killer whales in the workplace are unpredictable.

How Doctors for the Defense
Can Fudge Medical Reports

Naturally, doctors working for the defense try to submit reports that are clearly in favor of the defendant. Be aware of the tricks used by a defendant's doctors:

- Defendant's doctors will label Post-Traumatic Stress Disorder as mild depression to undermine the seriousness of your client's condition.
- Defendant's doctors conveniently (not mistakenly) misinterpret psychological test results because some symptoms for PTSD are the same as mild depression. They are deliberately seeking to trivialize your client's condition to minimize your client's compensation.
- Defendant's doctors' written reports will emphasize your client's mild depression and state that your client is a traumatized person who is merely depressed.
- Defendant's doctors can abuse the psychological tests. One psychological test requires the patient to answer numerous questions that have a built-in Lie Scale. If the Lie Scale is raised, that means the client may be trying to give the expected answers.

Some doctors for the defense will claim that an increase in the Lie Scale indicates that the client is lying and therefore the client's account of the injury could be a lie. What this really means is that the test could be lying—not your client. Doctors should not administer or interpret psychological tests, as this is the work of properly trained psychologists. Psychologists and doctors have completely different training, so beware of a doctor for the defense attempting to interpret psychological tests.

Sharks in the workplace should never be confronted alone.

Jellyfish in the workplace float in a pack and attack together.

Legal Argument

Coral in the workplace are bonded together with corporate
t-shirts, caps and logos and feed of living creatures.

Defining injury

Kendell (1975) stated that mental illnesses carried intrinsic biological disadvantages. The DSM IV, the psychiatrist's bible, states, "There is much physical in the mental disorder and much mental in the physical disorder." Sanders and Keshavan (1998) reported that most of the signs of a neurological examination in adult psychiatry can be reliably evaluated and that many have been validated against techniques such as the EEG.

If your client is being subjected to psychological stress in the workplace, it is likely that the employee will suffer from panic attacks. These panic attacks are defined by the tachycardia exceeding ninety beats per minute, experiencing dry tongue/mouth, sweaty palms and/or the extremities of the body, cold clammy skin, skin pallor, pupillary dilation, tremor and fluctuations in blood pressure with wide pulse pressure. These physical signs are psycho physiological correlates of acute anxiety and subsequently of panic attack and disorder.

Accordingly, the research of Kutas and Federmeier (1998) states . . . *Some of the same brain areas take part in both bodily regulation and the cognitive processes creating an indirect relationship between the mind and the body that may bear on how various psycho physiological measures are to be interpreted.*

Stress makes the body age faster according to recent tests performed by Elizabeth Blackburn at the University of California. The special enzyme, telomerase, which is pivotal in the aging process, works by protecting the end of chromosomes called telomeres that gradually wear away in normal aging. Professor

Blackburn and her team found that severely stressed people have extreme wear and tear to their telomeres. These details should be inserted into your Statement of Claim—and of course, you will be asked for particulars so you will require specialists' reports.

Alligators in the workplace hide and wait for victims.

International Covenant on Economic Social and Cultural Rights (ICESCR)

All civil servants worldwide will have similar Harassment Guidelines. If your client is an Australian public servant, the defense will use the following from the Australian Public Service Commission and insist that the management only gave your client feedback:

Workplace harassment must not be confused with legitimate comment and advice (including relevant negative comment and feed back) from managers and supervisors on the work performance or work-related behavior of an individual or group. Feedback on work performance or work-related behavior differs from harassment in that feedback is intended to assist staff to improve work performance or the standard of their behavior.

Australian Public Service Commission
Eliminating Workplace Harassment Guidelines

Your client is entitled to quiet enjoyment in the workplace and any form of bullying/harassment in the workplace is an issue of workplace health and safety working conditions. Safe and healthy working conditions are enshrined by the United Nations, and Australia, as well as many other countries, is a member of the United Nations. Workplace injuries caused by bullying and harassment result from unsafe and unhealthy working conditions.

However—if your client was bullied/harassed in any government department worldwide, use Article 7 of the ICESCR. The government would be in breach of its United

Nations obligations if nothing was done for your client. Of course, your client would have informed those at the top of the organization of the bullying/harassment and not be side-swept to a harassment awareness officer to deal with the problem. More often than not, those acting in that capacity are the problem, as they do not understand the mechanics of what is really going on or the consequences. Harassment awareness officers are usually attached to human resources. Their job is to ensure that employees have mandatory training and do not make waves by going to top management. In fact, it is forbidden in large organizations for employees to speak to top management. However, I have been reliably informed that those who venture to a government minister are given priority attention. The words said to me were "everyone jumps when a minister gets a complaint." Alleged contravention of Article 7 in your Statement of Claim will embarrass the government employer of your client and give a greater impetus to your media release. This will also raise your profile as a defender of employee rights.

International Covenant on Economic, Social, and Cultural (ICESCR)

Article 7

The States to the present Covenant recognize the right of everyone to the enjoyment of just and favorable conditions of work which ensure, in particular:

(a) Remuneration, which provides all workers, as a minimum, with

(i) Fair wages and equal remuneration for work of equal value without distinction of any kind, in particular women being guaranteed conditions of work not inferior to those enjoyed by men, with equal pay for equal work

(ii) A decent living for themselves and their families is accordance with the provisions of the present Covenant

(b) Safe and healthy working conditions
(c) Equal opportunity for everyone to be promoted in his employment to an appropriate higher level, subject to no considerations other than those of seniority and competence
(d) Rest, leisure and reasonable limitation of working hours and periodic holidays with pay, as well as remuneration for public holidays

Note that it is enshrined in this United Nations document that section 7(b) states there should be safe and healthy work conditions. Use this section if your client is a civil servant working for a government. If there is harassment or workplace bullying, then that particular government is in breach of its United Nations obligations.

World Health Organization Act (Cth) 1947

Each member country of the United Nations will have an act that relates to the World Health Organization. In Australia, the World Health Organization Act (Cth) 1947 (chapter 1, Article 2) approved of Australia becoming a member of the WHO and Australia became a signatory.

The First Schedule of WHO Act 1947 states "Health is a state of complete physical, mental and social well-being and not merely the absence of disease or infirmity." The Act gives an obligation to Australia to attain the objectives of the WHO, which is for all people to attain the highest possible level of health.

The Constitution of the Commonwealth of Australia gives a presumption of validity, which is the fundamental rule of constitutional law. Workplace bullying/harassment and its subsequent injuries, therefore, contravene the WHO of which Australia is a signatory. Use this if your client is in the armed services, a public servant, or an employee of any other government organization. Remember, that those at the top must be made aware of the behavior and its consequences.

Australia is also a signatory of the Human Rights Charter, which can be compared with the Directives of the European Union whereby the European Parliament has stated that workplace harassment must be considered a health and safety issue. Victimization in any workplace is a form of violence. A person who is victimized in the course of employment has a legitimate grievance (Hall 1982). In 1996, WHO declared violence to be a major worldwide public health problem and identified four priority objectives for adoption, which should be implemented by organizations.

To describe the problem, *assess the nature and scope of the workplace problem.*

- To understand the problem, *analyze the origin of the problem.*
- To identify and evaluate possible interventions, *define the intervention relating to the analysis of the origins of the problem.*
- To disseminate knowledge and implement effective action, *use valid knowledge regarding action and intervention to manage and control workplace violence.*

The European Commission, DG-V, has accepted that equal emphasis be given to the damage caused by verbal assault, threats and intimidation for "incidents where persons are abused, threatened or assaulted in circumstances related to their work, involving an explicit or implicit challenge to their safety, well-being or health" (Wynne et al 1996).

Probable

Working conditions must be safe.

- Is your client's workplace safe?
- Is the workplace properly supervised to make it a safe workplace?

Lawyers for the defense will try to turn the word *probable* into *possible*. Medical reports for your client must always use the word *probable*.

In the case of *Rogers v Brambles Australia Ltd* (1998) 1 Qld R 218, the judge stated that if the doctor said that the plaintiff would probably be able to return to work, allowances must be made for the risk that the plaintiff would not be able to do so. Therefore, the compensation was increased.

Your client's doctors' reports should include the following information:

- It is probable that the injuries are caused by the workplace.
- It is *probable* that the injuries prevent a return to work.

The following examples provide some idea of what is happening in the community. Additional examples are listed at the end of this manual:

- A young soldier hung himself at Singleton Army Barracks after being subjected to prolonged abuse and bullying.
- A 15-year-old girl in the Air Training Corps committed suicide after being accused of fraternizing with a 29-year-old instructor.
- A young Aboriginal soldier committed suicide because of racism and bullying.
- A Greek soldier was found, after three days, hanged at Sydney's Holsworthy Barracks. His body was scrawled with the words "Spic and Spiros" and a beard had been sketched onto his chin to mock his Greek heritage. No one noticed he was missing. His parents did not believe he committed suicide.
- Soldiers from Townsville's Lavarack Army Barracks dressed as the Ku Klux Klan to intimidate, bully, and taunt soldiers who had dark skin.
- In South Korea, a 22-year-old soldier who had been persistently bullied opened fire on fellow soldiers.

In each of these cases, it is probable that the deaths resulted from bullying—not a mere possibility. Avoid the word "possibility" like the plague.

Reasonable

Defense lawyers will try to state that the actions of management were "reasonable."

Stroud's Judicial Dictionary gives the word "reasonable" the *prima facie* meaning of reasonable in regard to those circumstances of which the actor called on to act reasonably knows or ought to know. In the Australian context, *Opera House Investment Pty Ltd v Devon Building Pty Ltd* (1936) 55 CLR 110 declared reasonable to mean reasonable in all the circumstances of the case.

The dominant principle of Australian industrial law that applies in cases of discipline, dismissal, demotion, appraisal, retrenchment, etc is one of fairness. In essence, it is the Australian concept of a "fair go": *Jackson v Work Directions Australia Pty Ltd* (1998) 17 NSWCCR 70.

In *Buxton v Bi-Lo Pty Ltd* (1998) 16 NSWCCR 234, Walker J. concluded that only if the employer's action in all circumstances was fair could it be said to be reasonable and that in deciding the issue of fairness, he applied an objective test of the reasonable observer in all the circumstances of the case.

I cannot stress the importance of the Events Chart. This documents consistent workplace bullying behavior that your client has endured. Simply verbalizing events could be perceived as whining or being unable to cope with *reasonable management directives*.

It has now been established from the case of *Attorney General's Department v K* (2010) NSWWCCPD 76 that there is no requirement at law that a worker's perception of events must pass some *qualitative test of reasonableness* in order to establish an entitlement to compensation.

The worker, in this case, based her perception upon real events that happened at work. It was found that it did not matter if the worker's perception was erroneous or irrational. The court only had to determine if the events at issue actually occurred and, if they did, whether the worker's injury resulted from those events. In other words, the worker does not have to establish that his/her perception of events was rational. The worker only has to establish that the events in question occurred and that the injury flowed from a genuine reaction to those events in order to succeed.

This case is like manna from Heaven for injury lawyers. Get going on the Events Chart and include your client's perception of the events. Remember, the events must have actually happened, so include witnesses, times, and dates on the Events Chart.

Foreseeability

Note what Justice Mason said of "foreseeability" in *Council of the Shire of Wyong v Shirt* (1980) 146 CLR 40:

. . When we speak of a risk of injury as being foreseeability, we are not making any statement as to the probability or improbability of its occurrence . . .

He also stated that a risk that is unlikely to occur *could* be a foreseeable risk. This means that if there is any risk of your client being injured by a workplace situation that is not likely to happen, it can still be considered "foreseeable" that your client would be injured.

If your client has been bullied in the workplace and suffers from Post Traumatic Stress Disorder as a result, then your client's employer can see this as a foreseeable risk. Note the bullying events on the Events Chart for your client's doctor.

The case of *Council of the Shire of Wyong v Shirt* (1980) 146 CLR 40 was referred to by Kirby J. in *NSW v Fahy* [2007] 232 CLR 486 where he stated that the case of *Shirt* correctly states the law. For the purpose of deciding whether a breach of duty has been established, the High Court has encouraged all those in a relationship of "neighborhood" (and certainly employers) to keep in mind to act upon the affirmative obligations of accident prevention that can sometimes arise out of the particularities of the relationship in question.

It doesn't matter how the injury is described—only that an injury would occur.

"Reasonable foreseeability" is subjective; therefore, there has to be a general standard of susceptibility. It must be shown that any person going through the systematic bullying in the shoes of your client would suffer an injury, which makes that a foreseeable injury.

The mere fact that your client is in employment gives the required relationship of proximity—*Jaensch v Coffey* (1984) 156 CLR 549.

Aquatic snakes in the workplace are poisonous.

Negligence

Workplaces must have safe work policies. This means that a culture of bullying/harassment will not be tolerated. In *McLean v Tedman* (1985) 155 CLR 306, the Court stated that an employer has an obligation to "establish, maintain and enforce . . . a safe system of work."

If there is no training policy on acceptable work culture and behavior, then your client's employer is negligent. Having an anti-bullying policy alone is not enough for a defense. There must be training on the workplace policy or the organization must bear liability for any workplace incidents that have injured your client.

Allowing a culture of bullying to flourish in the workplace is negligence. Your client's employer is under a duty of care to avoid causing your client personal injury. In *Page v Smith* [1996] 1 AC 155, Lord Browne-Wilkinson stated that "it matters not whether the injury . . . is physical, psychiatric or both—and that any distinction between physical and psychiatric injury is artificial and outmoded."

However, be aware that in nervous shock cases such as *Tame v NSW* (2002) 211 CLR 317, unless the defendant knows that the plaintiff is peculiarly susceptible to psychiatric damage, the defendant is entitled to assume that the plaintiff is a person of normal fortitude. The risk of injury must be a foreseeable risk, which is real and therefore foreseeable.

It is important that you state that your client has *not* suffered from an infliction of pure psychiatric injury and that your client undergoes medical tests that substantiate that the client has *physical injuries* caused by an unsafe unhealthy workplace. Insist on the following tests to substantiate physical injury and make sure that any findings are linked to the injuries suffered by workplace bullying/harassment directed to your client:

- EEG—the electroencephalography that is the registration of the electrical potentials recorded by an electroencephalograph
- Magneto encephalography
- Position emission tomography
- MRI—magnetic resonance imaging
- Eye tracking
- Pupillary/cardio measures

It was held in *Mt Isa Mines v Hopper* [1997] EQC 92-879 that management has an ongoing responsibility to educate all staff about workplace policies and to provide ongoing training that is up-to-date. The employer must ensure that the policies are relevant and must demonstrate a real commitment to those policies. It was established that a plaintiff would succeed if that person proves that the defendant employer has not ascertained the plaintiff's health and safety at work.

Historic Negligence to Use in Your Argument

Use the following cases and weave your argument around them by relating the events and actions of the defendant to fit what has already been established in case law:

Negligence is a careless state of mind: *Filliter v Phippard* (1847) 11 QB 347.

The employer is liable for damages for injuries from negligence: *David v Britannic Merthyn Co* [1909] 2 KB 164.

. . . Omission to do something, which a reasonable man, guided upon those considerations, which ordinarily regulate the conduct of human affairs, would do, or doing something, which a prudent and reasonable man would do: *Blyth v Birmingham Waterworks Company Co.* (1856) 11 Ex 781.

. . . Take reasonable care to avoid acts or omissions which you can reasonably foresee would be likely to injure your neighbor: *Donoghue v Stevenson* [1932] AC 562.

In 1856, Alderson B said: "Negligence is the omission to do something which a reasonable man, guided upon those considerations which ordinarily regulate the conduct of human affairs, would do, or doing something which a prudent and reasonable man would not do." This case was referred to by Gleeson C. J. in *NSW v Fahy* [2007] 232 CLR 486. Reasonableness is the touchstone, and considerations of foreseeability and risk avoidance are evaluated in that context.

In *Jones v Dunkel* [1958-59] 101 CLR 298, it was established that in order to have an action of negligence for death or personal injuries your client must do the following:

- Have evidence
- Ensure the evidence is positive in pointing to negligence
- Make sure that the evidence arises from circumstances that caused the injuries and that it can be proven.

A grievance procedure and complaints data should be on file. Subpoena these records. Once the court awards damages at common law for a breach of contract and/or negligence, the damages can include interest on any money that is already paid out or lost as a direct result of the defendant's breach of contract and/or negligence: *Hungerfords v Walker* (1989) 63 ALJ 210. This is legislated in most jurisdictions.

There must be a well-publicized system of commitment to receiving and resolving clashes at work. Justice Dodds held this in *Carlisle v Council of the Shire of Kilkivan and Brietkreutz,* District Court of Qld No. 12 of 1992.

Employer obligations are as follows:

- To supply a training manual on workplace behavior
- To use the manual in formal training
- To have ongoing training—not a one-off
- To have a grievance procedure that is genuine
- To record all complaints

In relation to your client who is suffering stress, the High Court in *NSW v Fahy* referred to *Barber v Somerset County Council* [2004] 1 WLR 1089. A schoolteacher suffered psychiatric injury from work-related stress. The House of Lords applied as a standard of negligence "the conduct of the reasonable and prudent employer, taking positive thought for the safety of his workers in the light of what he knows or ought to know."

Negligent Recruitment and Retention

Negligent recruitment is emerging as a tort that seeks liability against the employer where an employee is improperly hired and ultimately causes injury to another employee (Schneid et al 1997). This was first developed in the United States where the courts determined that employers had a duty to exercise reasonable and ordinary care in the employment and selection of careful and skilful co-employees. This has been expanded by the courts to include that an employer can be liable for the injurious acts of an employee if those acts were not only within the scope of the employment, but also outside the scope of employment and the employment setting. The US courts now hold employers responsible for failing to screen and evaluate individuals before offering employment.

The US case of *Yunker v Honeywell, Inc.* 496 N.W. 2d 419 (Minn. Ct. App. 1993) was the first case to address the issue of workplace violence due to negligent hiring. For the first time, the court made the distinction between the negligent hiring theory and the negligent retention theory.

The court noted that negligent hiring focuses on the adequacy of the employer's pre-employment investigation of the employee's background. The *Yunker* case exemplifies the trend in the US to permit recovery for victims of workplace violence.

Negligent retention is closely allied to negligent hiring. The above case of *Yunker* defined negligent retention as focused "on when the employer was on notice that an employee posed a threat and failed to take steps to insure the safety of their parties." *Yunker* could add an interesting arm to the argument.

Duty of Care

Duty of care exists as a balance to negligence. In *Grant v Australian Knitting Mills Ltd* [1936] AC 85, Lord Wright states: *All that is necessary as a step to establish the tort of actionable negligence is to define the precise relationship from which the duty to take care is to be deduced.*

Your client is owed a duty of care and a necessary relationship exists in which the employer owes the employee a duty of care in the workplace. Therefore, it is axiomatic that the *concept of a duty of care, as a pre-requisite of liability in negligence is embedded in our law.*

When an employee is injured in the workplace due to bullying/harassment, the simple question then arises: Did the employer fail to discharge a duty owed to the employee in all the circumstances of the case to exercise reasonable care in order to obviate the dangers of injury to which the employee was exposed?

Metropolitan Gas Co v City of Melbourne (1924) 35 CLR 186, states, "No conclusion can be reached until first the mind conceives affirmatively what should be done." Therefore, it is appropriate to note the following actions that could have caused an injury:

- Failing to carry out adequate inspections of the workplace when management has been made aware of a workplace grievance in respect to workplace bullying/harassment.
- Failing to arrange investigations by an appropriate qualified person when an employee has filed a grievance.

- Failing to ensure that the provisions of the relevant Workplace Health and Safety Acts were complied with by the organization.
- Failing to instruct all employees as to the risk of injury as a result of exposure to bullying/harassment in the workplace.
- Failing to arrange a system by which it was ensured that appropriate qualified personnel followed up on any reports of bullying/harassment.
- Failing to act upon such reports.
- Failing to institute adequate training and policies and ensuring training has been conducted to make all employees aware of the organization's policy and training programs with regard to workplace bullying and victimization.

It must always be proved that the injuries were a result of a breach of duty of care. In *Hamilton v Nuroof* (1956) 96 CLR 18, it was held that an employer's duty to its employees is a duty to take reasonable care to avoid exposing the employees to unnecessary risk of injury. Muir J. also considered the principle in *McLean v Tedman* (1985) 155 CLR 306 whereby an employer's obligation is to establish, maintain and enforce . . . a safe system of work. This case imposed a standard of care where employees would be protected from exposure to risk of injury by the employer's negligence or negligent work practices.

In *Zammit* [1998] QSC 150, Muir J. held that the risk of an injury such as post-traumatic stress disorder was foreseeable by the employer:

. . . Having regard to the evidence, it is plain that there was a foreseeable risk of psychiatric injury to the plaintiff if appropriate measures were not taken to minimize his exposure to stress . . . a reasonable man in the position of the defendant would have foreseen that his conduct involved a risk of injury to the plaintiff or to a class of person including the plaintiff which was not far fetched or fanciful.

Furthermore, his Honor found that, given that the employer could foresee the risk, the employer's conduct fell short of the standard of care that would be exercised by a reasonable man in the position of the employer: The risk of psychiatric and physical injury to the plaintiff at all times was substantial.

The defense, in this case, argued that employing clinical psychologists for the purpose of providing counseling was evidence of established measures taken to deal with employee stress.

Nevertheless, it was held to be inadequate to dispense of the employer's duty of care and referred to *March v E & MH Stramare Pty Ltd* (1991) 171 CLR 506 that the defendant's breach of duty was "so connected with the plaintiff's loss or injury that, as a matter of ordinary common sense and experience, it should be regarded as the cause of it."

A duty of care is mandatory in the workplace. In *Arnold v Midwest Radio* [1999] QCA 20, Mrs. Arnold suffered a psychiatric breakdown from being victimized by her employer. Mrs. Arnold, thirty-seven, claimed damages for alleged personal injuries received as the result of her employer's breach of duty of care. The employer, *Townsville Independent News* was vicariously responsible for the alleged actions of her boss; therefore, her employer was alleged to have breached its non-delegable duty towards her. Mrs. Arnold described the actions of her boss, which caused her to suffer depression, phobic anxiety, and panic, resulting in serious psychiatric consequences and a claim filed by her for breach of Workplace Health and Safety.

Her employer, Mr. Williams was alleged to have engaged in the following behavior:

Constantly using foul language to Mrs. Arnold and other staff

- Persistently using abusive language to Mrs. Arnold and other staff
- Regularly threatening to dismiss Mrs. Arnold
- Falsely accusing Mrs. Arnold of intending to take proceedings for sexual harassment against another member of the staff
- Boasting that he could reduce women to tears
- Cutting off Mrs. Arnold's access to long distance calls
- Refusing to pay Mrs. Arnold's car allowance—even though it was part of her employment
- Constantly refusing to advise or assist Mrs. Arnold when she requested advice in making decisions
- Criticizing Mrs. Arnold's advice to customers— baseless criticism directed at customers who bought advertising space in the *Townsville Independent News*
- Arranging for the newspaper not to pay Mrs. Arnold commission for selling advertising space
- Refusing to give Mrs. Arnold leave of absence to visit her de facto husband's dying father
- Displaying an insensitive attitude towards Mrs. Arnold's distress after the death of her de facto husband's father
- Creating an atmosphere of tension and frustration in the workplace based on actions taken
- Falsely accusing Mrs. Arnold of engaging in criminal activities
- Asking Mrs. Arnold if she could procure someone to commit a murder
- Constantly using abusive, foul language during weekly staff meetings

Even though some of the behavior was directed at other members of the staff, the judge concluded that the established evidence could be applied to Mrs. Arnold based on witnesses who noted deterioration in Mrs. Arnold during her working time.

The judge determined that the negative treatment given Mrs. Arnold was not justified, that there was a breach of duty owed to Mrs. Arnold, and that her condition was a result of the breach of duty owed by the employer. The judge also stated that Mrs. Arnold was entitled to succeed in her case based on her employer not providing a safe system of work, which resulted in Mrs. Arnold sustaining a psychiatric injury during the course of her employment.

The judge noted that the employer did not produce any evidence of a system at work (such as workplace policies and training) that would have ensured that employees were not subjected to the kind of treatment they endured. Furthermore, the company took no reasonable steps to ensure that such intolerable treatment of the employees was addressed.

The judge determined that Mrs. Arnold would probably not be able to return to the workplace although there was some likelihood that her health could improve in the future. She was awarded $572,512.87 in damages. However, on appeal, the court determined that it was up to Mrs. Arnold to prove that the alleged incidences caused her psychiatric injury. Since she had not kept records, she was unable to prove this. Also, her past and future economic losses were unsubstantiated based on never having been in full-time employment—Oh dear! If only she had the Events Chart!

However, this is an important case in workplace bullying. The trial judge admitted evidence of bullying based on complaints by other employees of stress, tension, and uncertainty in the workplace. He said: *In a case like this, where evidence establishes a course of conduct generally towards her and other members of staff . . . she is entitled to rely upon such incidents even though they were not directed towards her personally.*

The court did not accept the defendant's claim that tough measures were called for because of a financial crisis in the business. The court stated that "the treatment . . . could not be justified by the most generous assessment of the parameters within which a reasonable managerial prerogative might be exercised."

Crimmins v Stevedoring Industry Finance Committee (1999) 74 ALJR 1 held that:

The common law imposes a duty on the employer because the employer is in a position to direct another to go in harm's way and to do so in circumstances over which that employer can exercise control. The duty is, of course, not absolute: it is the duty of a reasonably prudent employer and it is a duty to take reasonable care to avoid exposing the employees to unnecessary risks of injury.

The duty extends to taking reasonable steps in accident prevention and not waiting for accidents to happen before safeguarding the health and safety of employees. Sprigelman C. J. in *Crimmins* noted that: *The laws of negligence is concerned with human beings. It is not concerned with specific occupations.*

Use this case if you have a defendant who maintains that a particular occupation differs from the mainstream and, therefore, the same rules don't apply.

Duty, to whom it falls to discharge it, is that of a reasonable prudent employer, and it is a duty to take reasonable care to avoid exposing the employees to unnecessary risks of injury. An employer's required degree of care and foresight must naturally vary with the circumstances of each case (see *Hamilton v Nuroof* (1956) 96 CLR 15.) Where there is a fault of omission, that is, the employer did not take steps to prevent the workplace injuries, Dixon C. J. and Kitto J. stated in *Hamilton* that:

It is absolutely necessary that the proof of that fault of omission should be one of two kinds, either—to shew (sic) *that the thing which he did not do was a thing which was commonly done by other persons in like circumstances, or—to shew* (sic) *that it was a thing which was so obviously wanted that it would be folly in anyone to neglect to provide it.*

The breach of duty of an employer to provide a safe system of working is a duty that rests on an employer personally and that if it is not provided, his liability, even if the fault is that of a servant or an agent, is a breach of his own duty and not a breach of other employees. However for a liability to occur, there must be negligence on the part of the employer to other employees. It is the duty of the employer to provide a safe system of working. If all the employees are denied training in harassment awareness and there is no workplace policy in this area, then there is negligence by the employer to provide a safe system of working.

The Supreme Court in *Doherty v NSW* [2010] NSWSC 450 found that employers must ensure that there are adequate systems in place to avoid harm to employees and that those systems are effectively implemented. Mr. Doherty was a former crime scene investigator who was exposed to traumatic crime scenes after being diagnosed with post-traumatic stress disorder and depression without receiving appropriate treatment for his condition. He was awarded $753,676 damages, but this was reduced by 35 percent because he failed to disclose his symptoms and take reasonable care for his own mental health.

Practicable

"Practicable" necessitates the court to determine the following:

- Risk of injury
- Employer's awareness of the risk
- Costs to eliminate the risk.

By having a grievance procedure, there is the element of awareness. It is the sole duty of management to maintain safety.

In *Nimmo v Alexander Cowan & Sons Ltd* [1968] AC 107, Lord Upjohn stated:

It is not merely the fact that doing what is necessary to maintain safety is more within the knowledge of management, but, not only the sole power, but the sole duty to make the place of work comply (with the law) rests upon management . . . it is the duty of the employer to make the place safe so far as is reasonably practicable. It is his duty with his experts to consider the state of the place of work in all its circumstances and to take whatever steps he can, so far as reasonably practicable, to make it safe. He must know and be able to give the reasons why he considered it was impracticable for him to make the place safe. If he cannot explain that, it can only be because he failed to give it proper consideration, in breach of his bounded duty to the safety of his workmen.

The High Court in *Chugg v Pacific Dunlop Limited* (1990) 170 CLR 249 referred to *Nimmo*. The Court held that the definition of "practicable" must be answered by a consideration of the means by which a risk can be removed or mitigated. If a requirement or procedure is not complied with, the only issue is whether it is practicable. It is likely that defense lawyers will say that eliminating bullying is not practicable. However, the High Court in *Chugg* held that "practicable" in s4 of the Occupational Health and Safety Act 1985 (Vic.) requires some consideration of the question of foreseeability. Use this decision for foreseeability to explain why employers cannot rely on workplace training not being practicable.

Barnacles in the workplace are found in shallow and deep water. They have been there a long time. Don't interfere.

Breach of Contract

There is an implied term in the contract between your client and the employer that states your client will be working in a safe environment. A breach of contract exists when that environment is not safe, your client is a victim of constant bullying/harassment, and the employer ignores the situation.

The mere fact that your client works for someone establishes a contract. In *Perkins v Grace Worldwide (Aust) Pty Ltd* (1997) 72 IR 18, the Full Industrial Relations Court held that:

Trust and confidence is a necessary ingredient in any employment relationship. That is why the law imports into employment contracts an implied promise by the employer not to damage or destroy the relationship of trust and confidence between the parties, without reasonable cause.

In *Bliss v South East Thames Health Authority* (1987) ICR 700, the court stated that if the employer requires that the employee submit to a psychiatric examination when there is no reasonable grounds, then that is a breach of contract. Furthermore, *It was an implied term of the plaintiff's contract that the Authority would not without reasonable cause conduct itself in the manner likely to damage or destroy the relationship of confidence and trust between the parties as the employer and the employee.*

This case was used in *Baltic Shipping Company v Dillon* (1993) 176 CLR 344. These two significant cases show that there must be a relationship of trust and confidence in a contractual situation—i.e. the employment—where there is bullying, there is no trust and confidence.

It was stated in the case of *Post Office v Roberts* (1980) IRLR 347 that an inaccurate appraisal also exposes the employer to liability or a breach of contract. Many victims of bullying/harassment are bullied into signing an inaccurate appraisal.

The workplace has a duty of care to ensure that your client is not injured. These duties are non-delegable. The employer must take full responsibility for the workplace and not rely on supervisors or others.

A breach of duty of care exists if the employer fails to do the following:

- Carry out adequate inspections of the workplace when made aware of a workplace grievance regarding workplace bullying/harassment.
- Arrange investigations by an appropriate qualified person when your client makes a grievance.
- Ensure that the provisions of the workplace health and safety legislation were not put into effect. All democratic countries have similar legislation to the workplace health and safety legislation in Australia.
- Instruct all employees as to the risk of injury as a result of exposure to bullying/harassment in the workplace.
- Arrange a system to ensure that an appropriate qualified person follows up reports of bullying/harassment.
- Act upon such reports.
- Institute adequate training, policies, and continuing training with regards to workplace bullying/harassment.
- Implement a system that ensures all employees were made aware of the organization's policy and training programs regarding workplace bullying/harassment.

Lord McMillan stated in *Bourhill v Young* [1943] AC 92 that:

The duty to take care is the duty to avoid doing or omitting to do anything... ... (that would cause) *. . . probable consequence injury to others.*

The Court in *McLean v Tedman* (1985) 155 CLR 306 held that the workplace has a duty to provide a safe system of work and that extends to maintaining and enforcing it.

In *Mt Isa Mines v Hopper* [1997] EQC 92-879, it was stated that it is not enough for a defendant workplace to state that anti-bullying/harassment policies were in place and that every employee was given a copy. There is an ongoing responsibility for workplaces to educate all staff about those policies and to provide effective and ongoing workplace training. Policies must be monitored as well as ensuring that they are up to date and relevant and to demonstrate a real commitment to workplace health and safety.

It is no defense for the employer to use the Nuremberg defense and say the supervisor was responsible or that the responsibilities were delegated.

In *Kondis v State Transport Authority* (1984) 154 CLR 672, it was held that the employer has the exclusive responsibility for the system of work to which he subjects this employee and that the employee has no choice but to accept and rely on the employer's provision and judgment.

If an employer insists that your client has to acquire a new skill that is so ridiculous and unreasonable for the job, then that is workplace bullying and a breach of contract: *Cresswell v The Board of England Revenue* (1984) 2 All ER 713.

If your client is employed because he/she has the necessary qualifications then is undermined and humiliated for not having other qualifications, that is bullying and a breach of contract: *Printing Industry Employees Union of Australia v Jackson & O'Sullivan Pty Ltd* (1958) 1 FLR 175.

Bullying by Appraisal

Work is a contract.

In *Tymshare Inc v Covell* 727 F2d 1145 (1984), Scalia J. concluded :*The doctrine of good faith performance is a means of finding within a contract an implied obligation not to engage in the particular form of conduct, which in the case at hand constitutes "bad faith."*

Scalia J. also held that the contract itself would indicate the content of the duty in the sense that it is imbued or infused with the obligation not to engage in particular conduct.

It is a general contractual term that the parties agree to do an action that requires the concurrence of both the employer and employee and that each will do all that is necessary for carrying out that particular action. Whether or not it is in writing, it is implied that the parties to the work contract will do all that is necessary to facilitate the action that forms part of the contract. If the employer fails to provide adequate training and subsequently dismisses an employee, then that employer could be regarded as breaching the contract. In the case of *Auckland Provincial District Local Authorities v Mt. Albert City Council* (1989) NZILR 651 it was held that:

It is also an implied contractual term in employment that the appraisal system used is carried out by a qualified person and is not derogatory, unduly intrusive, or offensive to the employee. A mismanaged appraisal system could make the employer liable for defamation, negligence, and a breach of statutory duty. However, that is not to say an adverse but accurate appraisal report cannot be written. There can be an adverse but accurate appraisal but the information must only be communicated to the necessary personnel and not used for general workplace gossip. The employer must not make broad allegations that cannot be sustained about the conduct of an employee.

It is essential that an adverse appraisal is only communicated to the necessary personnel and not used for general gossip. Furthermore, the employer must not make broad allegations that cannot be substantiated about the conduct of an employee. It is paramount that there is procedural fairness in the appraisal system.

In *Earl v Slater & Wheeler Ltd* (1973) 1 All ER 145, the Court held that failure to follow procedure was held to be procedural unfairness and therefore it could be reviewed.

A lack of proper procedure in appraisals amounts to bullying and denies the employee a safe system of work. The workplace has a duty to provide a safe system of work, which extends to maintaining and enforcing it. Therefore, in order to maintain a safe system of work, the workplace is obliged to not only enforce a safe system of work—that is a workplace without bullying—but also to maintain a safe system of work by providing workshops and training in awareness of bullying/harassment.

Proving Injuries Resulting from Workplace Bullying/Harassment

Lord Reid in *Rahman v Arearose Ltd* [2001] QB 351 stated that the employee must prove a case by the ordinary standard of proof in civil actions and that . . . *he must make it appear at least that on a balance of probabilities the breach of duty caused or materially contributed to his injury.*

This is an important case for your client. Make sure that the medical professionals state on their medical reports that "on a balance of probabilities, the breach of duty caused or materially contributed to (your client's) injuries"—and quote this case in court. Injuries from bullying never manifest immediately; therefore, it is unlikely that a victim would identify the exact time and circumstances for when the injury began.

However, one should consider the opinion of Lord Reid in the Scottish case of *Gardiner v Motherwell Machinery and Scrap Co Ltd* [1961] 1 WLR 1424 where he considered conflicting medical evidence at length. He stated:

In my opinion, when a man who has not previously suffered from a disease contracts that disease after being subjected to conditions likely to cause it, and when he shows that it starts in a way typical of disease caused by such conditions, he establishes a prima facie presumption that his disease was caused by those conditions.

This case is essential for your case if your client has not previously suffered from the depression and anxiety that was caused by workplace bullying.

The Court in *Comcare v Moori* (1996) 132 ALR 690 held that conditions involving a disturbance of the normal functions of the body and mind are within the term "disease" and therefore are defined as "injuries" under the Safety Rehabilitation and Compensation Act (Cth) 1988.

"Disease" is defined in section 4 to mean any ailment or aggravation of such an ailment suffered by an employee, being an ailment or aggravation that was contributed to in a material degree by the employee's employment.

Ailment is defined as any physical or mental ailment, disorder, defect, or morbid condition (whether sudden or gradual).

Injury is defined by section 4 of the Safety Rehabilitation and Compensation Act (Cth) 1988 as a disease suffered by an employee of a physical or mental injury (other than a disease) or an aggravation of a physical or mental injury (other than a disease) arising out of, or in the course of, the employee's employment.

In cases arising from injuries due to workplace bullying/ harassment, the defense will undoubtedly argue that the plaintiff has failed to prove a connection between the injury and the work. Lord Reid in *Gardiner v Motherwell Machinery and Scrap Co Ltd* [1961] 1 WLR 1424 dispels that argument. These are the essential elements in an *Action of Negligence*:

- A duty to take reasonable care which is owed by the defendant to the plaintiff
- A breach of that duty by failure to satisfy the expected standard of care
- Damage to the plaintiff from that breach or failure

Once negligence has been shown to exist, then the plaintiff must show that the defendant's negligence caused the injury. In other words, prove that the damage to the plaintiff resulted from the defendant's breach or failure. In order to show that the defendant's negligence caused the plaintiff's injury, the plaintiff must show the following:

- How the accident happened. That is, detail the bullying/ harassment events and how and when they occurred and identify the subsequent damage and injuries.
- Identify the defendant's conduct on the balance of probability, which caused or materially contributed to the injuries.

By linking the defendant's negligence to the injury suffered by the plaintiff, the Australian courts embark on a two-tiered inquiry factual and attributive causation. These two elements must be satisfied when determining whether the defendant's negligence was the cause of the plaintiff's injuries.

Factual causation requires the plaintiff to prove that the defendant's negligence in fact caused the plaintiff's injury. The "but for" test applies. Would the plaintiff's injuries have been suffered "but for" the defendant's negligence?

Attributive causation determines whether the defendant's negligence (acts or omission) "was so connected with the plaintiff's loss or injuries that as a matter of ordinary common sense and experience it should be regarded as the cause of the injury." *March v Stramare (E&MH)* (1991) 171 CLR 506.

In *Wilsher v Essex Area Health Authority* [1987] QB 730, Mustill L. J. made this statement of principle:

If it is an established fact that conduct of a particular kind creates a risk that injury will be caused to another or increases an existing risk that injury will ensue; and if the two parties stand in such a relationship that the one party owes a duty not to conduct himself in that way; and if the first party does conduct himself in that way: and if the other party does suffer injury of the kind to which the risk related; then the first party is taken to have caused the injury by his breach of duty, even though the existence and extent of the contribution made by the breach cannot be ascertained.

In *Farrelly v Qantas Airways Ltd* (2001) 22 NSWCCR 331, Bishop J. held that to establish that the employment concerned was a substantial contributing factor to the injury concerned, it is sufficient to establish that the injury arose in the course of the worker's employment and that there was some causal connection with the employment of a lesser degree than what is required to establish that the injury arose out of it. The court also found that if the relevant injury is found to arise out of the worker's employment, then the employment concerned must be a substantial contributing factor to such injury. The defendant's conduct must materially contribute to the injury.

In the case of *Batiste v State of Queensland* (2002) QdR 119, the Queensland Court of Appeal held that it remained the law of negligence for a plaintiff to prove that the defendant's conduct materially contributed to sustaining the injury. Make it a major and substantial cause of the injury backed up with medical reports.

But For Test

This raises the question—would the plaintiff have been injured "but for" the negligence of the defendant?

The following cases show that when using the "but for" test, the court often incorporates policy considerations when coming to its conclusions.

In *McKierman v Manhire* (1977) 17 SASR 571, a woman was knocked over by a car. The woman was found to be 20 percent negligent and the driver 80 percent negligent. The woman was admitted to hospital. She went to take a phone call at the hospital office and fell over a step. Although the fall at the hospital could not be linked to the car accident, the hospital was negligent in failing to warn her of the step. The woman was not guilty of contributory negligence of the second accident.

In *Pyne v Wilkenfield* (1981) 26 SASR 441, a woman was injured as a result of the negligence of the driver of the car and, as a result, had to wear a cervical collar. While wearing the collar, she tripped on a footpath because her vision was restricted. It was held that the second accident arose causally from the first accident. The woman was not guilty of contributory negligence. The driver of the car was liable for the results of both accidents.

As the "but for" test is problematic particularly where there is more than one cause of an injury, the courts have added an extra criteria to determine whether the defendant's negligence should be attributed as the cause of the plaintiff's injury. This attributive aspect of causation is referred to as the common sense test.

The "but for" test has proven to be inadequate or troublesome and can yield unacceptable results that must be tempered by the making value judgments and infusing policy considerations.

Factual causation is now determined by the "but for" test—but for the negligent act or omission, would the harm have occurred? *Adeels Palace Pty Ltd v Anthony Moubarak* (2009) 239 CLR 420. Therefore the words "but for" would look excellent on your client's medical reports. You can then refer to *Adeels Palace Pty Ltd v Anthony Moubarak.* In *Adeels Palace*, the High Court identified factual causation as an element in the Civil Liability Act 2002 (NSW) section 5D(1) (factual causation) which is to be determined by the "but for" test—but for the negligent act or omission, would the harm have occurred? Jurisdictions in all democratic countries cover this aspect of negligence in either case law or legislation.

Causal Connection

Identify the causal connection between your client's injuries and the bullying/harassment at work. *Hoffmueller v Commonwealth,* [1981] 54 FLR 48 stated:

If a defendant does an act for the purposes of precipitation the symptoms apt to flow from persecution paranoia or an existing anxiety situation, no doubt the necessary causal relation may be found. Where he acts knowingly of the possibility that symptoms will be precipitated, or carelessly disregarding that they may be more difficult questions will arise.

Your client's injuries must be linked to workplace bullying/ harassment. The defendant will be liable for your client's injuries if the defendant is the *cause* of the injuries. Remember, the workplace must be a material or substantial or major cause of the injury. Look at the legislation in your state or country. It will give you the exact words and this should be used in the medical reports.

The causal connection can be either an *act* or an *omission* by the employer. Your client must show that there *was* a practical means of ensuring an absence of injury.

The test for causation is a question of fact—make sure you client is completing the Events Chart regularly.

- The facts must be referred to with common sense
- The facts must relate to experience
- The facts must involve considerations of policy judgments
- The facts must have value judgments.

Your client must show that injuries were "caused or materially contributed to" by the employer's conduct: *March v Stramare Pty Ltd*. The courts use this test of causation whether the judgment is founded on contract or negligence. The workplace injuries are a breach of your client's work contract and negligence on the part of the employer in failing to provide a safe workplace.

The test in *March v Stramare Pty Ltd* was not examined by the High Court in *Adeels Palace Pty Ltd v Anthony Moubarak*. The High Court noted that section 5D(1) Civil Liability Act 2002 (NSW) (CLA) was a departure from the common law position, but the Court did not give a different result. This is discussed further in Statutory Framework below in relation to causation and duty of care as defined in this legislation. Use this when linking your client's injuries to the workplace culture and behavior.

Justice Thomas admitted in *Hawthorne v Thiess Contractors Pty Ltd* [2001] 401 QCA 223 that the authorities on causation are in a very unsatisfactory state in Australia and even though he noted that low level of connection could suffice to prove damages for personal injuries, His Honor said that it's impossible to identify that level. Stay on the safe side, make a strong link of causation between the workplace and your client's injuries, and make the link unbroken. There is now factual causation and scope of liability.

Excessive Workloads

This is a common complaint by victims of bullying/harassment.

Koehler v Cerebos (Australia Pty Ltd) (2005) HCA 15 will be used by lawyers for the defense. In this case, the plaintiff was retrenched then re-employed part-time with the same workload. The court held that none of her complaints suggested that she was experiencing any difficulties that affected her health. The court also stated that a reasonable employer should not have to identify a psychiatric injury as a result of overwork and stress. The employer was entitled to assume that the employee would be able to perform his/her duties in the absence of evident signs of warning of the possibility of psychiatric illness.

Look at the case of *State of New South Wales v Seedman* [2000] NSWCA 119. Seedman, a police officer with little training, was thrust into child abuse work. She didn't complain because of the police macho culture. The police department knew of the stress associated with this type of work and already knew how to incorporate systems of work to avoid the consequences. There was also a great deal of literature on the topic; subsequently the police department could not claim it had no idea what was going on. It was easily proved that there was a foreseeable risk of harm to Seedman who was exposed to the worst-case scenarios at work. Acting Justice Meagher said there was no distinction as to whether the injury was physical or mental.

If your client's employer had anti-bullying/harassment policies, then that is evidence that acts of bullying/harassment would cause foreseeable injuries.

In *Sinnott v F J Trousers Pty Ltd* [2000] VSC 124 the worker, a computer operator, was exposed to excessive stressors, long hours, and pressures at work. His employer gave him no technical support or assistance and took no notice of his complaints. The plaintiff developed a major depressive illness and/or adjustment disorder. The judge noted the following regarding the employer:

- Required the worker to keep working
- Knew that the worker was having difficulties coping
- Knew that the worker was at risk of having a mental illness or breakdown
- Kept the worker working in a position of danger (excessive workloads)
- Failed to take adequate precautions for the worker's safety

The judge was highly critical of the employer who said that that the worker was not entitled to recover from purely a mental illness. The judge noted that it was a startling proposition from the employer as it meant that the employer was really saying: *Although the employer cannot break the body of an employee during the course of his employment, nevertheless, it is permitted to break the mind at will irrespective of the circumstances.*

Excessive workloads can also be attributed to not being trained properly for the job, which leads to being bullied/harassed because things aren't done properly—no matter how hard your client has worked.

Your client should make all injuries as a result of the workplace conditions known to the employer. Look at what happened in the case of *Queensland Corrective Services v Gallagher* (1998) QCA 426. The Qld Court of Appeal held that "upper management" has to be informed. Never mind the harassment officer appointed by Human Resources—that is useless and merely a ploy to protect the organization from litigation.

How Large Organizations
Trick Employees into Not Litigating

All large organizations such as the public service, banks, hospitals, energy companies, and ambulance services have a system in place that is really designed to prevent or deter employees from litigation. This came about from *Queensland Corrective Services v Gallagher* (1998) QCA 426.

Gallagher was a security guard at a jail. He became depressed based on his working conditions and suffered workplace injuries as a result of the bullying culture. His supervisor knew of his depression. He took the Queensland Corrective Services to court and won over $500,000 because the Court held that he suffered depression and his employer did nothing about it. However, the Queensland Corrective Service appealed. You can imagine the furor that would result for employers, particularly the government, if that decision stood. I had just been admitted to the bar and the buzz was that this *had* to be overturned for policy reasons. Well, of course, it was and the reason given was that Gallagher did not make his injuries known at "the top." This is important for your client based on the decision of the court:

- There was no evidence the employer might reasonably foresee the plaintiff would be injured.
- There was no evidence that the injury was caused by negligence during employment.

The most important aspect of *Gallagher* was that those at the top did not know. This was where the case fell over. Your client must inform the person at the top, and if nothing is done, then your client can confidently pursue the road to compensation.

As a consequence of *Gallagher*, large organizations in Australia now have harassment safety officers. These are either volunteer employees or staff from human resources who are tasked to assist a person who is feeling unsafe in the workplace. Furthermore, there are constant training sessions to provide educations on anti-bullying/harassment policies that are compulsory and instigated by human resource departments. Of course, when employees are first inducted into the organization, they are told in no uncertain terms that if they have a grievance, they can only go to a certain person—the person directly above them or the harassment safety officer. Employees are forbidden to go to the top. This directive bullies the employee into not reporting the problem, because once the top is made aware of the bullying/harassment and nothing is done, then the organization attracts liability.

The first thing you must do when you get a new client who has been suffering from workplace bullying/harassment is to let their organization's upper management know. This means the CEO, the government minister, the head of the department—the top means the top. After that, if nothing is done about it, then your client is on a winning streak—*Gallagher's case*.

Your client must report that the bullying/harassment happened during the course of employment. Include in your statement the events and the injuries and emphasize the foreseeability of your client being injured by the organization in allowing irrational and dangerous behavior in the workplace.

Corporate Responsibility

Some suggest that it is difficult to prosecute corporate bodies for criminal offenses because of the inherent individualism of the criminal law (Fisse et al 1988). The difficulty is to establish the necessary intent of *mens rea* in the corporation for the relevant offenses from the directors, managers, or even employees of the corporation (Crabtree 1994). *Mens rea* can be established by an entrenched culture and, therefore, validates behavior that causes injuries.

In Australia, the law does recognize corporate responsibility for criminal behavior. In England, the law has identification or alter ego theory of corporate liability. Pursuant to this, the Court seeks a natural person "who is . . . the directing mind and will of the corporation, the very ego and center of the personality" of the corporation: *Lennard's Supermarkets Ltd v Asiatic Petroleum Co Ltd* [1915] AC 705. If that person has the necessary *mens rea,* it is attributed to the corporation.

A corporation . . . must act through living persons, though not always one or the same person. The person who acts is not speaking or acting for the company. He is acting as the company and his mind which directs his acts is the mind of the company . . . If it is a guilty mind, then that guilt is the guilt of the company: Tesco Supermarkets Ltd v Nattrass [1972] AC 153.

The concept of "directing mind or will" was approved by the High Court in Australia in *Hamilton v Whitehead* (1988) 82 ALR 626. In this case, the respondent, a managing director of a company, was held to actually be the company and that his mind was the mind of the company. The company liability was direct, not vicarious. Mason C. J., Wilson, and Toohey J. J. found that the respondent, therefore, was knowingly concerned about the commission of the offenses committed by the company. Their Honors agreed with Lord Reid in *Tesco Supermarkets Ltd v Nattrass*. Lord Reid in Tesco explained the significance of direct liability rather than vicarious liability.

I must start by considering the nature of the personality, which by a fiction the law attributes to a corporation. A living person has a mind, which can have knowledge or intention or be negligent and he has hands to carry out his intentions. A corporation has none of these: it must act through living persons, though not always one or the same person. Then the person who acts is not speaking or acting for the company. He is acting as the company and his mind, which directs his acts, is the mind of the company. There is no question of the company being vicariously liable. He is not acting as a servant, representative, agent or delegate. He is an embodiment of the company, one could say, he hears and speaks through the persona of the company, within his appropriate sphere, and his mind is the mind of the company. If it is a guilty mind then that guilt is the guilt of the company. It must be a question of law whether once the facts have been ascertained, a person in doing particular things is to be regarded as the company or merely as the company's servant or agent. In that case any liability of the company can only be statutory or vicarious liability.

Their Honors in *Hamilton v Whitehead* agreed with Bray C. J. in *R v Goodall* (1975) 11 SASR 94 101.

. . . the company, being a legal entity apart from its members, is also a legal person apart from the legal personality of the individual controller of the company, and that he in his personal capacity can aid and abet what the company is speaking through his mouth or acting through his hand.

As the saying goes—fish go rotten from the head down!

Compensated Injuries Resulting from Cluster Bullying

Cluster bullying/harassment is a lot of little acts, which cause serious injuries. I have included this section to inform your client that every little act is significant in the big picture and must be recorded on the Events Chart.

In *Di Barrista v Comcare* (1996) AAT (unreported) No.V94/25, the supervisor caused a stress-related incapacity based on his behavior toward Mr. Barrista by acting in the following manner:

- Told Mt Barrista that he was going to get rid of certain people.
- Made personal comments about Mr. Battista that were not work related.
- Complained that Mr. Battista worked too hard, was too conscientious, and should relax more, while trying to appear to be caring and helpful—this is a common scenario.
- Undermined Mr. Battista.
- Crossed Mr. Barrista's name off distribution lists before Mr. Battista had seen the material.
- Changed Mr. Battista's first name, Sab, to Sad on internal documents.
- Asked Mr. Battista for examples of his touch-typing ability—his job did not require typing.

The Tribunal clearly indicated that the supervisor's behavior was about power, and that Mr. Barrista's stress-related incapacity was brought about by the supervisor's workplace behavior. Mr. Battista received compensation because workplace bullying/harassment was causing his stress-related incapacity.

In *Brooks v Comcare* (1995) 38 ALD 612, the employee was found to have suffered "from a phobic state, resulting in stress and anxiety when in the proximity of his former supervisor."

After a back injury, Brooks returned to work and to a deteriorated workplace relationship with his supervisor. He lodged a complaint but was later called into his supervisor's office where he was told: *You can't fight City Hall. Wayne, if this takes more than ten minutes of my time to dispatch or dispose of, you're dead.*

It is highly significant that the Tribunal recognized that power played a major part in the bullying, and the victim got compensation for suffering and anxiety.

In *Mobb v King Island Council* (1994) (unreported) Industrial Relations Court of Australia, VI 2246, Ms. Mobb was subjected to intense pressure and a degree of obstruction in her attempts to perform her duties. She was also subjected to a campaign of harassment, rumors, and innuendo. Subsequently, she became ill. The Court found the employer to be vindictive and a disgrace, because Ms. Mobb was a dedicated and hardworking employee whose boss dislike her demeanor and started harassing her and spreading innuendo in the workplace. Ms. Mobb won the case.

The following points are important to remember:

- Show the damages
- Link the damages to the bullying/harassment
- Show how it was foreseeable by management that bullying behavior would cause the injuries.

Torture Techniques

There are standard torture techniques in war. Whatever the war, Biderman's stages for torture are consistent and can be replicated in the workplace. I have included Robyn Mann's chart (1994) as a useful tool to use in your argument. In some instances, bullying is perceived as something weak people complain about. Assuredly, lawyers for the defense will pursue that line. Note the similarities between war torture and work torture. You can bring this into your argument—but of course, there must be a completed Events Chart.

BIDERMAN'S STAGES FOR TORTURE

Biderman's stages for torture and coercion	Abuser's actions	Victim's response
Isolation	Befriends the newcomer. Introduces to others with high praise. Monopolizes until other staff begin to reject. Warns of perils of associating with other members of staff.	Deprived of developing social support with colleagues. Initiates total dependence and acquires a false feeling of security. Confuses easily.
Monopolization of Perception	Informs victim through power alliances. Outlines superior knowledge and skills. Intimates that victim does not possess necessary knowledge and skills but may be able to acquire it through association with abuser.	Loses self-esteem. Doubts ability to perform. Self blames for accepting a position because of feeling unworthy. Consumed completely by introspective thoughts.

Biderman's stages for torture and coercion	Abuser's actions	Victim's response
Induced mental and physical exhaustion	Overburdens victim with time-consuming and/or physically demanding tasks. Places unrealistic standards of acceptance on these tasks.	Becomes physically and emotionally too weak to resist or challenge. Loses ability to reason rationally.
Threats	Reminds of power over victim's workload, promotional opportunities and acceptance in the hierarchy of the company.	Complies with demands to escape retribution. Displays anxiety about every action performed. Despairs of any change in the situation. Symptoms of depression.
Occasional indulgences	Praises victim's work in a public place.	Believes they have finally reached the accepted standard and that the pattern of abuse will stop. Begins to doubt that abuse really happened.
Demonstrating 'Omnipotence'	Exercises complete control over the victim who is taken for granted. Has 'read my mind' expectations. Accepts martyrdom for the company and of being indispensable to the company. Claims victimization by those who challenge abusive behaviour.	Accepts powerlessness. Accepts the pattern of behaviour by the abuser as normal.
Degradation	Spreads derogatory stories about the victim on work and personal topics.	Feels disgraced and humiliated. Loses all will to resist.
Enforcing trivial demands	Continues to remind victim through innuendo, suggestion and intimidating stories that the abuser's demands will be complied with.	Accepts habits of compliance.

This chart describes the pattern of victimization that begins succinctly and slowly develops into a reign of terror. Trauma by stealth is meant to impair the mind and encourage the victim to doubt self worth. These techniques have been used at all levels in organizations.

Octopus in the workplace will use one of
their arms to backstab.

Dismissal

If your client has left the workplace because of the bullying/ harassment, then that constitutes constructive dismissal. However, sometimes the workplace will have investigations that are not real but simply a smoke screen to cover legal loopholes. Smoke-screen procedures were noted in *Bostik (Aust) Pty Ltd v Gorgevski* [1992] 41 IR 452 by Justice Dodds:

- Employers' Procedural requirements must be real.
- Employers must genuinely investigate allegations of misconduct or neglect of duty or act of omission that might be grounds for dismissal.
- Employers must carry out a proper investigation and not merely go through the motions.
- Employers must look at mitigating factors (for example, past work records or future prospects).
- Employers must not use the court for its own investigation, as organizations must have their own proper procedures.
- Employers must not use actions that are harsh, unjust, or unreasonable.

An employer genuinely investigating an allegation of misconduct or neglect of duty, or some other act or omission, which might provide a ground for dismissal, is required to carry out a proper investigation and not merely go through the motions. The employer is required to ascertain whether there are mitigating factors, either associated with the alleged ground for dismissal, or arising from the employee's past record and future prospects. It is not intended that an employer should be able to substitute a court proceeding for its own investigation—i.e. to overcome procedural deficiencies by establishing to the satisfaction of the Court that the dismissal would not be harsh, unjust, or unreasonable on substantive grounds. Furthermore, a power to dismiss must be exercised other than harshly, unjustly, or unreasonably in both substantive and procedural senses.

Bullying/harassment is a form of molestation that has given your client vexation. Your client has the right to be free from molestation and vexation: *Baltic Shipping Co v Dillon* (1993) CLR 344.

Outfoxing *Tame*

The High Court decision in *Tame v New South Wales* [2002] 211 CLR 317 sent shivers down the spines of lawyers for the plaintiff in Australia. This was a policy decision to put the brakes on huge payouts. It was not medically correct and psychologists and psychiatrists were astounded that High Court judges would actually refer to a pure psychiatric injury. Psychiatrists and psychologists will tell you that this is incorrect terminology. The Australian High Court judges obviously had no psychological or neuroscience knowledge but, as lawyers we have to deal with their decision and outfox the rationale. Their fundamental position was to allow recovery for damages for pure mental harm if it could be reasonably foreseen that a person of normal fortitude might suffer harm in the circumstances of the case.

In *Tame,* the Court rejected established control mechanisms as definitive tests of liability. However, factors that gave rise to them may still be relevant to questions of reasonableness. The majority of the Court stated that the criterion of reasonableness imposed at all levels of inquiry (to determine the existence and scope of a duty of care, breach of duty, and damage) is an intrinsic control mechanism. The criterion of reasonableness sets boundaries in respect of liability for psychiatric injury and anchors the boundaries in principle, rather than allowing them to depend on arbitrary and indefensible distinctions.

A claim in respect of a psychiatric injury which is reasonably foreseeable is limited only by reference to general considerations: the compatibility of a duty of care with any conflicting professional responsibilities, whether imposed by statute or contract, and considerations of legal coherence. The question of what a reasonable employer should do as a response to a foreseeable risk of psychiatric injury to employees as a class or individually is subject to these general considerations.

You must emphasize the physical injuries that your client suffered due to workplace bullying/harassment. Your client's doctor must dispel any relationship of your client's injuries to pure psychiatric injury. Psychiatrists deny the notion of *pure psychiatric injury* anyway as there is a physical component, but they're not sitting on the High Court and are not arbitrators of what constitutes the law. Outfox *Tame* by hitting the physical injury button and use the brain scans of your client as visual evidence in court. Furthermore, refer to *Gallagher's* case (above). Remember, those at the top must be made aware of injuries. Your client should bypass the official harassment officer at the side of the organizational loop and go straight to the top.

Doctors should detail the status of your client's health and link any injuries directly to workplace bullying/harassment. An employer's duty to take care has to be performed in the light of the obligations on the employees to undertake stressful work. The doctors should examine the following symptoms:

- Heart palpitations
- Skin irritations and blotches
- Insomnia
- Anxiety—document in detail the actual physical injuries that are caused by anxiety
- Backache
- Stomach problems
- Bowel problems
- Nausea
- Migraines

107

- Endogenous depression—document in detail actual physical injuries associated with depression due to the workplace. Do not allow defense lawyers to trivialize this.
- Reduced gray matter density in the temporal cortex, which includes the hippocampus
- Increased perfusion in cingulate and paralimbic areas
- Reduction in altanserin uptake in the right hemisphere, which also includes posterolateral, orbitofrontal, and the anterior insular cortex
- Activation of the HPA axis, which involves stress neurotransmitters 5-hydroxytryptamine (5-HT) or noradrenaline (NA)
- Stimulation of the neurotransmitter system has resulted in CHR (corticotropin-releasing hormone) release from the hypothalamus and subsequent release of adrenocorticotrophic hormone (ACTH) from the anterior pituitary gland
- Spasms in the bowel
- Spasms in the bladder
- Dyspepsia from disordered contractions of the stomach
- Hypoglycemia (low blood glucose), which interferes with the function of the brain
- Changes in blood flow
- Stiff and sore muscles
- Increased tension of both agonist and antagonist muscle groups causing tremors
- Rapid heart rate and irregular heartbeats
- Activation of the sympathetic nervous system fibers
- Neurobiological disregulation
- Increased respiration
- Involuntary nervous system sympathetic discharge reactive to realistic fears

The following tests must be undertaken by your client to link injuries to the workplace

- Electroencephalography (EEG) registers electrical potentials recorded by an electroencephalograph
- Magneto encephalography
- Position emission tomography
- Magnetic resonance imaging (MRI)
- Eye tracking
- Pupillary/cardio measures

Moray eels in the workplace have sharp jaws and sharp teeth.

Events that Traumatize

The following events all happened in Queensland:

- A man working for an airline was poisoned when a workmate poured an ethanol-based liquid into his coffee.
- Workmates at a government organization poured urine into a colleague's car vents.
- A mock tombstone at a Halloween party had a worker's name on it, a culmination of other actions, which sent the worker into severe depression.
- A worker found a photo, in her pigeonhole, of her boss sitting naked on a toilet posing with a grin on his face. The caption said: *This is what I am going to do to you.*

Other workplace events by the foreman were not as traumatic but nevertheless subjected the victim to humiliating behavior.

In *Carlisle v Council of the Shire of Kilkivan and Briekreutz* (1995) Qld District Court No. 2/12/1995, Mr. Carlisle was subjected to the following:

- Harassed for eating an orange
- Called "stupid"
- Told he was of no use
- Ordered to perform menial tasks
- Ordered to undertake dangerous tasks
- Ordered to undertake unnecessary tasks

The Court found that because Mr. Carlisle had reported the behavior and nothing was done, the council was in breach of the following:

- Its duty to provide employees with a safe working environment
- Its contract of employment with Mr. Carlisle
- Its statutory duty imposed by the Workplace Health and Safety Act

The grouper in the workplace gives a powerful handshake to establish superiority.

Rescuers

When you read the horror true stories that I have included, you will note that many people are traumatized when a workmate commits suicide because of workplace bullying. The rescuer has a claim even if the rescuer did not witness the incident, and only assisted in its aftermath.

Under the Civil Liability Act 2002 (NSW), rescuers who sustain recognized psychiatric injuries after attending the site of a catastrophic incident caused by another's negligence may recover damages for pure mental harm (here we go again on the pure mental harm) from the negligent party. This was confirmed by the High Court of Australia in *Wicks v State Rail Authority of NSW* (2010) 267 ALR 23. Of course, by now you are aware that the injuries from such an event encompass biological injuries—so increase the amount of the claim for your client.

Conspiracy—When Two or More Persons Conspire to Injure a Person

Ganging up on a workplace colleague could be a conspiracy to injure. Look at the horror cases at the end of this book and you will see a plethora of cases where ganged up bullying caused severe injuries, long term disabilities, and even death. If this has happened to your client, then a criminal offense has occurred and you could bring in a conspiracy to injure. In these cases, you will probably require private investigators to collect the evidence. When two or more persons are animated by a desire to harm a person, it is considered a conspiracy to injure and is a criminal offense.

In *McKernan v Fraser* (1931) 46 CLR 343 the Court stated: *In an action against a set of persons in combination, a conspiracy to injure followed by actual injury, will have a good cause of action, and motive or intent when the act itself is not illegal is the essence of the conspiracy.*

Once it is established that two or more persons are bound together in their pursuit of injuring a person, anything said, done, or written by one of them to further the common purpose of injuring a person, will be admissible in evidence against the others. This is to prove to the court the participation of bullies to injure a person. It is also known as "combination" in criminal law, which means that bullies have combined to injure.

In *Sorrell v Smith* [1925] AC 700, the plaintiff must prove the purpose of the combination to be deliberately interfering with a man's trade, which is spiteful and malicious. Your client's use of the Events Chart is crucial here.

The co-conspirators rule in *Ahern v R* (1988) 62 ALJR 440 is the "rule which states that when two or more persons are bound together in the pursuit of an unlawful object, anything said, done, or written by one in furtherance of the common purpose is admissible in evidence against the others" for the purpose of proving an assertion or implied assertion contained in the act or declaration in question. The court added: *the combination implies an authority in each to act or speak on behalf of the others.*

Therefore, anything said or done by one conspirator in pursuit of the common purpose may be treated as having been said or done on behalf of another conspirator. Once participation in the conspiracy is established, the evidence would prove the nature and extent of the participation.

Note that the High Court in *Ahern v R* held: *The proof of conspiracy then, will typically be by way of circumstantial evidence of the words spoken, and acts done by the co-conspirators during its transaction.*

Bullying with intent to injure is criminal. Depending upon your client's situation, you may need to investigate a combination if there is a deliberate and malicious attempt to injure. This has happened in a number of bullying cases but your evidence must be watertight.

The crime of conspiracy was described in *R v Jones* (1832) 110 ER 485 as "either to do an unlawful act, or a lawful act by unlawful means."

To knowingly cause or allow behavior that causes workplace injuries is an unlawful act. In Australia, the common law of conspiracy is only in New South Wales and South Australia. The Commonwealth *Crimes Act* 1914 creates the statutory crimes of conspiracy. The Code States of Queensland and Tasmania have abolished common law conspiracy and replaced this with a statutory crime of conspiracy. The Western Australian Criminal Code (as amended in 1987) confines conspiracy to agreements to commit a crime. In the Australian Capital Territory, the Crimes

Act 1900 (NSW) was amended in 1988. The new section 349 creates statutory conspiracies, which incriminate agreements to commit an offense, to prevent or defeat the execution or enforcement of a law of the ACT to affect a purpose that is unlawful under a law of the Territory. The Northern Territory Criminal Code has enacted a number of statutory crimes for conspiracy. Your jurisdiction will have similar legislation and you can use these cases.

Lord Brampton stated in *Quinn v Leathem* (1901) AC 495 in reference to both criminal and civil conspiracy: *a grain of powder is harmful but a pound may be highly destructive.*

In the early Irish case of *Parnell* (1881) 14 Cox CC 508, Fitzgerald J. had earlier claimed that an agreement "to effect an injury or wrong" to a third party was an indictable conspiracy, even though its purpose, if executed, would in itself only ground a civil remedy, because this purpose "assumes a formidable or aggravated character when it is to be effected by the powers of combination."

Lord Bramwell stated in the civil conspiracy case of *Mogul SS Co Ltd v McGregor, Gow & Co* (1892) AC 25 that "a man may . . . encounter the acts of a single person, yet not be fairly matched against several." This statement was endorsed by Lord Esher MR. in *Temperton v Russell* [1893] 1 QB 715 and Lord McNaghten in *Quinn v Leathem*.

In general, the rules of evidence apply to the proof of criminal conspiracy. The only way conspiracy can be proved is by presenting direct evidence of the acts by which the alleged conspirators formed their agreement. Please bring in professional investigators if you are going down this road.

The Canadian Supreme Court in *Paradis v R* (1934) 61 CCC 184 stated:

No doubt the agreement . . . is the gist of the offense [i.e. conspiracy], but only in very rare cases will it be possible to prove it by direct evidence. Ordinarily the evidence must proceed by steps. The actual agreement must be gathered from "several isolated doings" having possible little or no value taken by themselves, but the bearing of which one upon the other must be interpreted; and their cumulative effect, properly estimated in the light of all surrounding circumstances, may raise a presumption of concerted purpose entitling the jury to find the existence of the unlawful agreement.

Ahern is now the leading Australian case dealing with the proof of conspiracy. Strictly speaking, the co-conspirators rule is an exception to the hearsay rule. Words and acts of the co-conspirators will be sought for admission, for their significance as physical and verbal acts, independent of their hearsay value.

The High Court in *Ahern v R* (1988) 62 ALJR 440 noted that conspiracies typically had to be proven circumstantially and by their reference to their overt acts. Once circumstantial proof was obtained, proof of acts by alleged co-conspirators can be relied upon for their non-hearsay value. Therefore, evidence can include one alleged conspirator's acts or declarations, which were not made in the presence of the others. These can be separate acts or words that would infer a combination. In this way, it is not hearsay and is *not dependent upon some circumstance to take it outside the hearsay rule, such as an implied authority making the acts and words of one the acts and words of the other.*

In *Tripodi v R* (1961) 104 CLR 1, it was stated that proof of the crime of conspiracy "may well consist in evidence of the separate acts of the individuals charged with, although separate acts, yet point to a common design and when considered in combination justify the conclusion that there must have been a combination such as that alleged in the indictment."

In *Ahern v R* (1988) 62 ALJR 440 the co-conspirators rule is that "rule which states that when two of more persons are bound together in the pursuit of an unlawful object, anything said, done or written by one in furtherance of the common purpose is admissible in evidence against the others for the purpose of proving an assertion or implied assertion contained in the act or declaration in question." The court added the "combination implies an authority in each to act or speak on behalf of others. Thus anything said or done by one conspirator in pursuit of the common purpose may be treated as having been said or done on behalf of another conspirator. That being so, once participation in the conspiracy is established, such evidence may prove the nature and extent of the participation . . . "

This is an important case to use where your client is a victim of ganged-up bullying and harassment in the workplace, which resulted in injuries.

Assessing Damages for Personal Injury Claims

The most basic principle governing an award of damages is that the plaintiff should receive a monetary sum that represents fair and reasonable compensation for the loss sustained by reason of the defendant's wrongful act. The courts have developed a number of basic principles governing the assessment of the quantum of common law damages. The following is a general guide depending on your jurisdiction.

In an action for personal injuries caused by negligence, damages are normally assessed from the date of the judgment. Types of damages will be considered. A claim for damages for personal injury will usually be made in contract, tort, or both and there will be a breach of some statutory duty. In common law, there is a distinction between the assessment of damages for breach of contract and damages in tort. Damages under tort and statute are designed to put the plaintiff in the position the person would have been in had the tort or breach of statutory duty not been committed. However, in contract, the court seeks to award a sum of money, which puts the plaintiff in the same position as if the contract had been performed. The court tries to give fair and adequate compensation.

Heads of damages: The courts will award compensatory damages in personal injuries for the following non-economic loss:-

- Pain and suffering
- Loss of amenities or enjoyment of life
- Diminished expectation of life

- Residual disfigurement—compensation for mental anguish and discomfort caused by the reaction of others to residual disfigurement.
- Mitigation of non-economic loss—if the injured person has refused medical treatment that would or might have diminished non-economic loss.
- Loss of earning capacity—this is not loss of earnings. Don't forget to include superannuation.
- Needs created by the injury—this includes gratuitous services of a domestic or nursing nature.
- Interest—payable on past economic loss dating from accrued cause of action to date of judgment
- Aggravated damages—the personal injury is caused by negligence
- Punitive or exemplary damages—intended to punish and make an example of the defendant and to deter others from similar wrongdoing.
- Collateral benefits—includes accident or disability insurance, private health insurance, sick pay, holiday pay, private benevolence, social security payments, Medicare benefits, workers' compensation payments.

There is an old saying in the sales industry—put your hand on the largest and most expensive—you can always come down but you can never go up. Think of this when preparing the claim for your client.

Australian Legislation and Policy

Occupational Health and Safety

The following refers to Australian legislation, but most jurisdictions in democratic countries will have similar laws relating to health and safety in the workplace. You can use the case law cited for sections in your jurisdiction's laws on workplace health and safety.

Part 3 of the OHS Act 2000 relates to the health, safety, and welfare of employees and other persons at a workplace.

Section 15—the employer's duty:

1. Every employer shall ensure the health, safety, and welfare at work of all the employer's employees.
2. An employer contravenes this subsection if the employer fails:

(2)(c) To provide such information, instruction, training, and supervision as may be necessary to ensure the health and safety at work of the employer's employees,

(2)(d) As regards any place of work under the employer's control:

(2)(d)(i) To maintain it in a condition that is safe and without risks to health,

(2)(e) To provide or maintain a working environment for the employer's employees that is safe and without risks to health and adequate as regards facilities for their welfare at work.

It is the employer who must ensure the health, safety, and welfare of employees at work. This obligation is a non-delegable duty: *Kondis v State Transport Authority* (1984) 154 CLR 672.

Note that the standard recognized by the common law, "to take reasonable care," is higher: *Kirk v Industrial Court (NSW)* (2010) CLR 531. The requirement is that the employer must ensure the health, safety, and welfare of employees or that persons are not exposed to risks to their health and safety at the place of work.

Time frame:

Section 49 part 6 states that the time frame for instituting proceedings for offenses is within two years after the act or omission alleged to constitute the offense. You must identify the risk to the health, safety, and welfare of employees and show how the employer has not discharged his/her obligations. Not having a workplace policy addressing harassment/bullying is an identifiable risk to workplace health and safety.

In all jurisdictions in democratic countries, the employer will have a defense in the legislation.

In NSW Australia, the employer's defense is found in section 53 OHS Act 2000:

Section 53 provides that: It shall be a defense to any proceedings against a person for an offense against this Act or the regulations for the person to prove that following:

- It was not reasonably practicable for the person to comply with the provision of this Act of the regulations the breach of which constituted the offense; or
- The commission of the offense was due to causes over which the person had no control and against the happening of which it was impracticable for the person to make provision.

Practicable:

The employer is obligated to take measures for the health and safety of employees and this is limited to taking such measures as were *practicable*. Lawyers for the defense will use this.

Note these sections in your jurisdiction within Australia. In *Kirk*, the Court stated that the High Court has held that these provisions place the onus upon the prosecution to show that the means, which should have been employed to remove or mitigate a risk, were practicable. If you are in Australia, the following are the relevant sections for your state or territory. This will be similar in overseas jurisdictions in democratic countries.

Occupational Health and Safety Act 1985 (Vic) ss 21,22
Occupational Health and Safety Act 2004 (Vic) ss 21,22,23
Occupational Health, Safety and Welfare Act 1986 (SA) ss 19,22
Workplace Health and Safety Act 1995 (Qld) ss 26,27
Occupational Safety and Health Act 1984 (WA) ss19, 21,22
Workplace Health and Safety Act 1995 (Tas) s9
Work Health Act (NT) s29
Workplace Health and Safety Act (NT) ss 55, 56, 57
Occupational Health and Safety Act 1989 (ACT) ss 27, 28
Work Safety Act 2008 ACT ss 14, 15, 21

The measures taken by an employer have to be *reasonably practicable*. The term is not defined in the OHS Act but may often involve a common sense assessment.

What must be done in connection with the health, safety and welfare of employees in the workplace depends upon the presence of identifiable risks and measures which could be taken to address them: *Kirk v Industrial Court (NSW)* [2010] CLR 531. Ask these questions.

1. What was reasonably practicable? I would say ongoing workplace training.

2. What was not reasonably practicable? The defense lawyers will use this, but remember—the employer's duty is *non-delegable.*

The employer's acts and omissions have to be identified. This is where faithful completion of the Events Chart is essential.

Bullying by Legislation

Provisions that could be detrimental to your client's safety at work are hidden in the Public Service Acts in Australian states and territories. For example, in Queensland, there is in section 85 of the Public Services Act (Qld) a provision whereby any public servant can be compelled to see a psychiatrist or doctor if the employer believes that the employee has a mental or physical problem. Rather than being used in the rare situation where the health of an employee would pose a threat to the workplace or public, this section, in some cases, could become the new toy for bullying/harassment. This section is a useful tool to silence professional staff and instill fear for expressing dissent within the workplace, which would cement the bully's power base.

Check the Public Service Acts in your jurisdiction and you will find the same provisions.

Bullying by a Government Department

It is expected that a complaint of bullying in a large public hospital would be handled sensitively. The following is a government response to a victim who was suicidal from the work-bullying situation at a large public hospital in Queensland. The victim was a highly skilled social worker with three university degrees. This letter is an insult and an example of sanctioned bullying.

I am in receipt of a report from the Investigations Officers appointed to conduct the investigation into allegations raised by you in your grievance. I am advised that a copy of this report was delivered to you on . . . (date) . . .

After giving careful consideration to all evidence available to me so far in respect of these allegations, I am giving serious consideration to implementing all recommendations contained in the report.

These recommendations are:

1. *You are actively performance-managed on each area where a deficit or difference is output is found compared to a reasonable workload of another (. . . work title . . . .)*
2. *That you be offered the services of the Employment Assistance Service.*
3. *That you be required to under go a medical examination to determine your ability to undertake the work you are engaged in;*
4. *That you be made accountable to the . . . team and that you acknowledge and action your professional*

accountability to the . . . Unit/Department and the senior (. . . rank . . .) of the team;

5. *That you acknowledge and action as appropriate all reasonable and lawful directives from your superiors (or line managers). If you fail to take such actions, disciplinary proceedings should be implemented*

6. *That (. . . the bullies names were inserted here . . .) be exonerated of all allegations*

7. *That the managers of all departments be reminded that they have a duty of care to their employees, especially with respect to unpaid overtime and supervision of work practice.*

In accordance with the principles of natural justice, no determination has been made, or will be made until you have had the opportunity to formally respond to the report and the recommendations.

Accordingly, you are required to reply to the report and the recommendations, in writing, that is by (.date . . .), by providing any material you wish to be considered.

If you do not respond, of if your response is received later than (. . . date . . .), I will make a decision on the material currently available to me.

In addition, I refer to my letter of (date.) in, which I offered you the opportunity to show cause why a proposed disciplinary penalty, a reprimand, should not be imposed. You were subsequently advised by e-mail from (. . . person. .) on (.date.) that you would be required to respond to this letter at the same time you responded to the Investigation Report.

The Employee Assistance Service offers a confidential counseling to all employees of . . . Department and you may wish to discuss with them your situation.

Note that the bullies were exonerated. This is a form of official bullying and would no doubt exacerbate your client's injuries at the thought of such an injustice.

Government Employee Bullied by the System

Warn your client that this can happen:

Madeleine (not her real name), a government employee in Canberra, collided with a government car at an intersection. She suffered neck and back injuries from whiplash. She was forced to sign a release stating private details and to confide information on issues that gave her stress to the so-called sympathetic caseworker assigned to her. This included problems related to her teenage children, which were subsequently revealed in court. Madeline was told that everything was confidential. However, her kids were made out to be delinquents and troublemakers and this was presented as the real reason for her stress—not the injuries from the car accident.

Madeleine also thought she was being rehabilitated by a caring occupational therapist. To her horror, when the case came to court, the so-called rehabilitation caseworker (whose employer was being paid by the insurance company) had reinterpreted her stress to be related to a demented personality with chronic disorders because of her children. Surprise, surprise—Madeleine was offered by way of compensation the *exact* amount to the dollar of her mortgage.

Her privacy was invaded so the insurance company had a benchmark to offer. The attitude was "She owes $$$$ so let's just offer her that." Madeleine struggles to this day from the trauma of not having been believed in court. She was made out to be a liar and defense lawyers vilified her children. Her son went on to be a war hero in Iraq and Afghanistan, and her daughter is now an executive in public service. Madeleine, however, developed cancer shortly after these events.

Tell your client to note the following:

- Never have a work interview alone if your afraid of the person conducting the interview.
- Ask permission to tape an interview—or have your lawyer present.
- If permission is refused, terminate the interview.
- Make a note of strange events—in Madeleine's case, she went for months putting up with phone calls at all hours of the night where the person hung up when she answered. This stopped after the case. Also, note the plate number of strange cars constantly parked outside the home. Bullying can occur in the system once your client makes a claim.

Overseas Jurisdictions

Heinz Leymann of Sweden was the first academic to identify workplace bullying as endemic in workforces throughout the world as he investigated the psychosocial work environment. In 1984, Leymann sought to identify the causes of bullying and the subsequent result of injuries attributed to workplace behavior. He placed the scientific origins of workplace bullying as Occupational Medicine rather than Occupational Psychology. As a result of his research, the Swedish government was the first country to legislate against bullying in the workplace.

The Swedish Government sought to improve the "person-environment" by introducing the Public Service Health Act (Sweden) No. 560 (1985) to recognize the detrimental effects of workplace health issues. This provided reference for a Swedish Commission on the Work Environment because of the government's concern about human suffering and the need to eliminate such phenomena from the labor market. The Swedish government offered financial incentives to management of organizations.

Accordingly, the Swedish Working Life Fund was set up by a decree of the Swedish Parliament to promote a healthy work environment and to establish active rehabilitation programs in the workplace. The Work Environment Act (Sweden) 1977 has been amended to encompass personal and occupational development for self-determination and occupational responsibility but does not enshrine legal rights for employees injured by deliberate workplace violence.

Following the Swedish legislation, the European Parliament stated that workplace harassment must be considered a health and safety issue and endorsed dignity as an approach to overcome harassment. The Presidency Conclusions of the Lisbon European Council 23 and 24 March 2000 instigated the establishment of guidelines for the Union to establish quantitative and qualitative indicators for translating the European guidelines on workplace dignity. Strengthening fundamental social rights became significant in adopting new directives in the field of employment. Using the powers conferred by Article 13(1) of the EC Treaty, the Commission introduced directives to forbid harassment and victimization and workplace behavior that is *violating the dignity of a person and of creating and an intimidating, hostile, degrading, humiliating or offensive environment*: Article 2(3) of the Race and Horizontal Directives.

In 1993, the Swedish National Board of Occupational Safety and Health brought in ordinances under the 1977 Work Environment Act to include explicit victimization at work.

In the Netherlands, the Working Environment Act 1980 was amended in 1996 to include provisions to prevent both psychological and physical aggression and violence in the workplace.

In the United States, the California Occupational Safety and Health Administration has issued guidelines on workplace violence that identifies workplace victimization causing a threat to health.

In 1996, the World Health Organization (WHO) declared that workplace violence is a major worldwide public health problem.

Statutory Framework

If your client is a public servant in NSW, note that Section 8 Law Reform (Vicarious Liability) Act 1983 (NSW) provides the following:

Notwithstanding any law to the contrary, the Crown is vicariously liable in respect of the tort committed by a person in the service of the Crown in the performance or purported performance by the person of a function (including an independent function) where the performance or purported performance of the function is as follows:

- In the course of the person's service with the Crown or is an incident of the person's service (whether or not it was a term of the person's appointment to the service of the Crown that the person perform the function) or
- Directed to or is incidental to the carrying on of any business, enterprise, undertaking or activity of the Crown.

For the purposes of this Act, a police officer is deemed by section 7 to be a person in the service of the Crown and not a servant of the Crown: (see *NSW v Fahy* [2007] 232 CLR 486).

Civil Liability Act (NSW) 2002 (CLA)

Your jurisdiction will have the equivalent of Civil Liability Act (NSW) (CLA) with almost the same provisions as New South Wales. I have referred to the NSW Act as the High Court provided important guidelines upon the interpretation of the CLA (NSW) in the application of duty of care and causation in *Adeels Palace Pty Limited v Anthony Moubarak* (2009) CLR 420.

The issue of duty of care was considered in *Adeels Palace* case by reference to s5B of the CLA.

5B General Principles

A person is not negligent in failing to take precautions against a risk of harm unless:

- The risk was foreseeable (that is, it is a risk of which the person knew or ought to have known), and
- The risk was not insignificant, and
- In the circumstances, a reasonable person in the person's position would have taken those precautions.

In determining if a reasonable person would have taken precautions against a risk of harm, the court is to consider the following (amongst other relevant things):

- The probability that the harm would occur if care were not taken
- The likely seriousness of the harm
- The burden of taking precautions to avoid the risk of harm

In *Adeels Palace Pty Limited v Anthony Moubarak* (2009) CLR 420, the High Court ruled that there was no breach of duty of care because the risk has to be a foreseen risk. Therefore, it is important that you stress in your Statement of Claim that the risk of injuries due to workplace bullying was a foreseen risk then refer to the High Court ruling in *Adeels Palace* that there is a breach of duty of care if the risk is a foreseen risk. Employing the wrong type of personality or not having suitable work policies and training would be a foreseeable risk that carried a risk of workplace injuries.

Causation As Defined by the High Court

In *Adeels Palace Pty Limited v An Anthony Moubarak,* the High Court dealt with causation and the provisions of the CLA, in particular section 5D.

Section 5D Civil Liability Act General Principles

A determination that negligence caused particular harm comprises the following elements:

- That the negligence was a necessary condition of the occurrence of the harm (factual causation), and
- That it is appropriate for the scope of the negligent person's liability to extend to the harm so caused (scope of liability).

In determining in an exceptional case, in accordance with established principles, whether negligence that cannot be established as a necessary condition of the occurrence of harm should be accepted as establishing factual causation, the court is to consider (amongst other relevant things) whether or not and why responsibility for the harm should be imposed on the negligent party.

If it is relevant to the determination of factual causation to determine what the person who suffered harm would have done if the negligent person had not been negligent:

- The matter is to be determined subjectively in the light of all relevant circumstances.

- Any statement made by the person after suffering the harm about what he or she would have done is inadmissible except to the extent (if any) that the statement is against his or her interest.
- For the purpose of determining the scope of liability, the court is to consider (amongst other relevant things) whether or not and why responsibility for the harm should be imposed on the negligent party.

You can see that section 5D(1) is divided in two parts—factual causation and the scope of liability. This is determined in applying the "but for" test—but for the negligent act or omission, would the harm have occurred? Your client's doctors' reports will establish that but for the workplace bullying, the injuries would not have occurred.

Although this is a departure from the common law position in *March v E & MH Stramare Pty Ltd* (1991) 171 CLR 506 that *causation is ultimately a matter of common sense,* the High Court did not come to a different result.

It is important to note that in *Adeels Palace,* the "but for" test of causation is alive and well. Use that in your case. This will be easy with your plethora of medical evidence.

The Workplace Health and Safety Act commenced on 1 January 2012 for the Commonwealth, Northern Territory Queensland, NSW and the ACT. A serious offense occurs where a person acts in a manner where they recklessly expose another to the risk of death or serious injury. The horror stories below will show you how serious workplace bullying is and how it can lead to s serious injuries and suicide.

Many bullied employees can be unfairly dismissed once it is known that that they are pursuing their rights. Under s394(2) of the Fair Work Act 2009 (Cth), unfair dismissal claims must be brought within fourteen days after the date of termination unless Fair Work Australia (FWA) is satisfied that there are *exceptional circumstances*:

- The reason for the delay
- Whether the person first became aware of the dismissal after it had taken effect
- Action taken by the person to dispute the dismissal
- Merits of the application
- Fairness between the person and other persons in a similar position.

This changes from the Workplace Relations Act 1996 (Cth) where the time limit was twenty-one days unless the applicant could show special circumstances.

A recent case of exceptional circumstances is *Shields v Warringarri Aboriginal Corporation* [2009] FWA 860 where Senior Deputy President Les Kaufman was of the view that the word "exceptional" meant that the hurdle for extensions of time was higher under the Fair Work Act than it was under the Workplace Relations Act.

Filling The Crevices with Common Law

A just interpretation of statutes is mandatory. A person does not voluntarily suffer injustice. It requires someone to do an injustice (Rawls, 1971) . . . *in a just society . . . the rights secured by justice are not subject to political bargaining or the calculus of social interests.*

For added impact, use this quote from Rawls when summing up your case—quite necessary if, like *Gallagher's* case, there could be serious policy considerations.

Every State and Territory has legislation concerning the workplace. Almost all jurisdictions in democratic countries around the world have legislation concerning the workplace. In Australia, your primary sources will be, for example, the Occupational Health and Safety Act NSW 2000 and the Workers' Compensation legislation of your state/territory.

The legislation details the employer's responsibilities. In each state/territory, the legislation tries to differentiate between physical and psychological injuries in relation to the criteria for compensation. Having read this manual, you are now aware that this area is not black and white —but you are now armed with more ammunition.

We will look at the NSW legislation as an example and you will find almost similar criteria in the legislation of your state/territory—or your overseas jurisdiction.

These are the key principles in the NSW legislation (Workers Compensation Act 1988 and Workplace Management and Workers Compensation Act 1998) :

- Objectives—to assist in securing the health, safety, and welfare of workers and in particular in preventing work-related injuries (s3)
- Liability—a worker who has received an injury (this includes psychological) shall receive compensation from the worker's employer in accordance with the Act (s9).
- For compensation to be payable, employment must be a substantial contributing factor to the injury. (s9A(1)).
- The fact that the injury arose out of in the course of the worker's employment does not necessarily mean that the employment was a substantial contributing factor. (s9A(3)(a)).
- A psychological injury will not be compensable if the injury was wholly or predominantly caused by reasonable action taken or proposed to be taken by or on behalf of the employer with respect to transfer, demotion, promotion, performance appraisal, discipline, retrenchment, or dismissal of workers or provision of employment benefits to workers. This will be used by the employer's lawyers, so keep it out of your statement of claim.

In *NSW v Fahy* [2007] 232 CLR 486 Kirby J. considered the enactment of legislation designed to re-express legal liability in negligence in ways intended to reduce such liability such as the *Civil Liability Act 2002* (NSW). Kirby J. stated that this is because common law operates in the crevices left after statutory provisions have addressed subjects on which the common law once spoke with uninterrupted authority. Where statute speaks, it is the parliamentary command that takes primacy and constitutes the starting point for legal analysis.

In other words, according to Kirby J., follow the legislation and then fill the gaps with common law.

Templates and Case Studies

Freedom of Information (FOI)

The object of the Freedom of Information Act 1982 (Cth) (the Act) is to extend as far as possible the right of the Australian community to access to information in the possession of the Government of the Commonwealth: s3(1). Other jurisdictions in democratic countries will have similar Acts whereby members of the public are able to obtain certain information unless that information is exempt or highly classified.

By section 11(1), subject otherwise to the Act, every person has a legally enforceable right to obtain access in accordance with the Act. Under s36(1). Subject to this section, a document is an exempt document if it is a document the disclosure of which under this Act:

- Would disclose matter in the nature of, or relating to, opinion, advice or recommendation obtained, prepared or recorded, or consultation or deliberation that has taken place, in the course of, or for the purposes of, the deliberative processes involved in the functions of an agency or Minister or of the Government of the Commonwealth and
- Would be contrary to the public interest.

Freedom of Information Application Template

The FOI Officer
Department
Address
City
State Post Code

To whom it may concern

In accordance with the Freedom of Information Act 1989 (ACT) [insert the appropriate Act for your state/ territory or Cth], I wish to be provided with the following information:

[Be specific about what you want or you could end up with 500 pages that you will not read]

[Do not generalize]—do not go on a fishing exercise—this is a waste of time and resources. You are more likely to get a positive response if you are specific].

Yours faithfully
Your name

If you are denied access to documents, under s58 of the FOI Act (Cth), the Administrative Appeals Tribunal has the power to review any decision that has been made by an agency of a Minister in respect of a request for disclosure under the FOI Act, and also to decide any matter in relation to the request that could have been decided by the agency or Minister.

The Tribunal (*Haneef and Department Immigration (The Tribunal* 2007) FCA 1273) will find for disclosure of information if:

- There is a general public interest in making information held by the Government accessible to the public
- A person or the general public is entitled to have access to documents containing decisions with affect them. Disclosure may reveal the reasons for the decision an
- The need for openness and accountability of the Department's operations.

In Australia, non-disclosure information is held to be for:

- Advice to Ministers, senior officers or free expression that would hamper the flow of advice from bureaucrats
- Disclosure would mean officers would be reluctant to record sensitive issues and
- Disclosure would inhibit full and frank discussions and may leave some people reluctant to record an opinion or provide advice.

Be aware of this when you send your request for information under the Freedom of Information Act.

Letter to Doctor Template

Dear Doctor . . .

Re: Brief for Mr./Ms. Workplace Victim's Report

To assist you with an overview of Ms. Victim's workplace situation, we have enclosed the Events Chart, which details the workplace events and the consequences of those actions. This will give you a "potted view" before you see Ms. Victim for the consultation.

As you are aware, the victim of workplace bullying/harassment has to prove a number of issues in order to succeed. The following are key things to remember:

- Phrases such as functional disability and clinical impairment are used throughout the report.
- Medical tests are explained in detail and the reasons for ordering them.
- Medical problems are explained scientifically.
- Speculation in your opinion is provided for the basis of the client's clinical profile. Using the word "probable" as opposed to the word "possible" is important. Lawyers and doctors for the defense will try to turn probable into possible to minimize the impact and relevance.
- In your opinion, would the workplace injuries have the same effect upon another person under the same conditions? This is important.

- Avoid using the words "emotional, emotional impulse, and frustration." Defense lawyers and doctors use these words as a tactic. In the case of *Thazine-Ayr v WorkCover (NSW)* 1995 12 NSWCCR 304, it was held that those words do not constitute an injury. However, these words will be repeated as a mantra by the defense because in the case of *Bahatia v State rail Authority (NSW)* 14 NSWCCR 568, Justice Burke stated that although post-traumatic stress disorder is a physiological injury, an emotional impulse is not.
- Injuries should be linked directly to events in the workplace.
- Use the words "but for." For example, would the client's injuries have occurred but for the (actions of the employer)? In the recent case of *Adeels Palace Pty ltd v Anthony Moubarak* (2009) 239 CLR 420, the High Court identified factual causation as an element to be determined by the "but for" test—but for the negligent act or omission, would the harm have occurred?
- Attribute the client's injuries to the negligence (acts or omission) of the employer.
- Detail evident signs that the client was suffering from the events in the workplace that should have been noticed by the employer.

Please find the Doctors' Diagnostic Chart below to assist you in writing your report on the injuries of Ms. Victim.

Doctors for the defense will undoubtedly attempt to dilute a PTSD to a mere mild depression. This is a common tactic, therefore, it is necessary to detail terminology for litigation purposes. This will also be a valuable aid for you when you are cross-examined in court and refer to your notes.

I have added the Doctors' Diagnostic Chart as, on many occasions, doctors who want to know exactly how to present their evidence for court have approached me. Keep it clear and succinct. The lawyers will apply the case law and legislation to fit the diagnosis.

Doctors' Diagnostic Chart

Description	Reason	PT SD Yes / no	Symptoms	Does it apply to the client?
Nervousness		Yes	On edge, tense, jumpy, easily startled, fearful	
Preoccupation with the trauma		Yes	Client talks a great deal about the events	
Pain / discomfort		Yes	Physical discomfort that appears disproportionate to the actual injury	
Sleeplessness		Yes	Insomnia, tiredness, fatigue	
Flashbacks and nightmares		Yes	Reliving the trauma in flashback, nightmares – similar emotional reactions as if the events were happening again	
Deterioration of performance		Yes	The client experiences an inability or difficulty in carrying our usual activities such as work, family responsibilities, social and recreational activities	
Phobia		Yes	Experiences fearfulness and avoidance of the place where the events occurred. Extreme apprehension associated with some activity related to the bullying/ harassment	

Description	Reason	PT SD Yes / no	Symptoms	Does it apply to the client?
Personality change		Yes	Withdrawn, moody, irritable, distracted, forgettable, unlike the usual self	
Dudgeon		Yes	Frequent unprovoked outbursts of anger with complaints about the carelessness of others and has a retributive attitude	
Detailing the events at work that caused the injuries	On the Events Chart	Yes	Link the injuries directly to the events in the workplace	
Feeling of fear of helplessness	On the Events Chart	Yes	Link directly to the workplace events	
Recollections are recurrent		Yes	Link directly to the workplace events	
Dreaming of the events – Repetitiveness of the dreams		Yes	Link directly to the workplace events	
Psychological distress to events	On the Events Chart	Yes	Link directly to the workplace events	
Physical reaction to the work environment	On the Events Chart – crying, vomiting etc	Yes	Link directly to the workplace events	
Have there been changes in symptoms			Link directly to the workplace events	
Heart palpitations	Link to the workplace		Due to fearfulness as a result of the workplace situation	

Description	Reason	PT SD Yes / no	Symptoms	Does it apply to the client?
Skin irritation and blotches	Link to the workplace		Associated with nerves due to the abuse and humiliation suffered. List the medication prescribed	
Insomnia	Link to the workplace		Due to anxiety about the persistent bullying	
Backache	Link to the workplace		Tension and feelings of anxiety due to the workplace situation	
Stomach and bowel problems	Link to the workplace		Related to the unpredictable nature of the workplace bullying/ harassment	
Lethargy	Link to the workplace		Associated with depression because of being undermined in the workplace	
Feelings of nausea	Link to the workplace		Sweating and shaking when the bullying/ harassment occurs. Can also occur when the bullying is 'honeyed' with false caring	
Migraine, severe headaches	Link to the workplace		Link to persistent bullying/harassment	
Murderous feelings and acute anger	Link to the workplace		Brought about by continuous bickering and undermining	
Constant feelings of irritability	Link to the workplace		Due to the inability to cope with the workplace situation	
No motivation	Link to the workplace		Got to the stage of 'why bother' in the workplace	

Description	Reason	PT SD Yes / no	Symptoms	Does it apply to the client?
Loss of self confidence and self-esteem	Link to the workplace		The sense of self worth is eroded and a loss of confidence to stand up to the bully.	
Prior injuries	What is the 'sudden change' to the existing condition? This needs to be identified.		Link this to the workplace events. Aggravations of a disease / injury must be linked to the workplace. Changes can be external or internal. List all the sudden and dramatic physiological changes or disturbances of the normal physiological state that occurred during the protected period of employment.	
Depression - To avoid the trivializing of this term, please detail the impact. This is necessary so that it is not seen as a 'mere mental condition'.	'Called endogenous depression because it is caused by some imbalance within the body's chemistry, rather than the result of a disappointment of loss…if not treated medically there is a significant risk of suicide.' *Dr William Wilkie,* Brisbaneç		Reduction of grey matter density in the left temporal cortex with will include the hippocampus in chronic depression. Increased perfusion in cingulate and paralimbic areas. A reduction in altanserin uptake in the right hemisphere, which also includes posterolateral, orbitofrontal and the anterior insular cortex.	

Description	Reason	PT SD Yes / no	Symptoms	Does it apply to the client?
Psychological stress This detail is necessary as the defence will be stating that the so-called bullying didn't happen, the client is a sensitive person, the client was having a period of emotional distress and that no one else complained so what is wrong? Further more, the mere mention of 'psychological stress' can have a connotation of 'mental distress', which could be trivialized by the defence lawyers and doctors.			*This involves the stress neurotransmitters 5-hydroxytryptamine (5-HT) or noradrenaline (NA).* *Stimulation of either of these neurotransmitter systems results in CHR (corticotropin-releasing hormone) release from the hypothalamus and subsequent release of adrenocorticotrophic hormone (ACTH) from the anterior pituitary gland.* O'Keene's (2000) *Evolving model of depression as an expression of multiple interacting factors,* **British Journal of Psychiatry, 177.** O'Keene identified different stressors which activate selective stress responses in the body but the most commonly activated of these systems is the hypothalamic-pituitary-adrenal (HPA) axis.	

Description	Reason	PT SD Yes / no	Symptoms	Does it apply to the client?
Anxiety This can be trivialized so it is necessary to detail 'anxiety' as having physical injuries. The para sympathetic nervous system opposes the effects of adrenaline and noradrenaline that are released during anxiety. As a result, there can be irregular contractions in the hollow organs in the body, which can result in irritable bowel symptoms or frequency of urination.	Link these injuries to the workplace situation		Changes in the blood flow Changes in internal organs Spasms in the lower oesophagus Tension headaches Chronic headaches Stiff and sore muscles in the neck and upper shoulders. Increased tension of both agonist and antagonist muscle groups causing tremors and the shakes. Backaches and pains in the chest because the chest muscles cannot rest easily. Increased rapid heart rate resulting in flutters and palpations due to occasional irregular heartbeats. The abdominal beats are a consequence of the increased irritability of the heart caused by activation of the sympathetic nervous system fibres.	

Description	Reason	PT SD Yes / no	Symptoms	Does it apply to the client?
'Impairment' Use this word frequently throughout the report.	A loss of use or derangement of any body part, or organ system, or organ function. *Guides to the Evaluation of Permanent Impairment,* 5th edition, 2002, at 2 and 601.		To damage or weaken something, especially in terms of its quality or strength. Chambers 21st Century Dictionary, 1999, reprinted 2004, Chambers AAT. Any loss of abnormality of psychological, physiological or anatomical structure or function. Taber's *Cyclopedic Medical Dictionary.*	
Panic attacks	A panic attack is a physical injury.		The tachycardia exceeds 90 beats per minute, dry tongue/mouth, sweaty palms and/or the extremities of the body, cold clammy skin, skin pallor, pupillary dilation, tremor and the fluctuations in blood pressure with wide pulse pressure.	

Description	Reason	PT SD Yes / no	Symptoms	Does it apply to the client?
'Foreseeable'	In your opinion, was it fore see able that the workplace events would have caused injuries to the client?		If the client has been bullied in the workplace and suffers from PTSD as a result, this can be a 'foreseeable' risk by the employer. 'Reasonable foreseeability' is subjective therefore there is a general standard of susceptibility. In your report, indicate if any person going through the systematic bullying in the shoes of the client would suffer an injury. This then becomes a 'foreseeable' injury.	
Never use the term 'pure psychiatric' injury. Medical tests must be ordered to establish that the client suffered physical injuries from the bullying and harassment.			Tests: EEG 1. Magnetoencep halo-graphy 2. Position emission tomography 3. MRI 4. Eye tracking 5. Pupillary/cardio measures. These finding must link the client's injuries to the workplace events.	

Description	Reason	PT SD Yes / no	Symptoms	Does it apply to the client?
Heart condition	If you suspect that the client could be at risk of a heart attack due to the workplace bullying, please order the necessary tests such as an electro-car diogram. List the detected injuries that can be attributed to the workplace events.		Workplace bullying can induce identifiable physiological changes. Dr Raftos, St Vincent's Hospital Sydney, stated that *acute emotional stress can result in identifiable physiological changes increases in pulse rates and blood pressure and these, depending upon the stimulus and upon the recipient, may be absolutely maximal. This could be the hardest work the heart does.*	
Cancer			There are studies currently being conducted around the world linking cancer to stress, and in particular, to workplace bullying. You may wish to pursue this if you think it relevant to the client's case.	

156

For your information, lawyers and doctors for the defense will use the following tactics:

- Label PTSD as mild depression to undermine your report
- Conveniently, misinterpret psychological test results to minimize compensation
- State that the client is a traumatized, sensitive person who is merely depressed.
- Use the built in Lie Scale on the psychological test to state that the client is only giving expected answers and that the client is lying
- State that the client's lack of promotion or work benefit is the real reason for mild depression—lack of promotion or losing work benefits are not considered bullying
- State that the client's thinking was irrational
- State that the client had a misperception of actual events
- State that the client rationalized past innocuous events that led to the illness

If you diagnose Ms. Victim with *severe depression*, you may wish to refer to Stouthard's Netherlands Study, as on a scale from 0-1, severe depression is classified as 0.65 to 0.80. This is on the same level as disseminated breast cancer and moderately severe brain injury resulting in permanent impairments and extreme intellectual disability.

Stouthards's study classifies *moderate depression* as 0.30—0.40 which is the same scale as multiple sclerosis in relapsing-remitting phase, severe asthma, chronic hepatitis B infection with active viral replication and deafness.

For your further analysis, if you wish to pursue this, go to http://eurpub.oxfordjournals. We feel that if your diagnosis of Ms. Victim were either severe or moderate depression,

Stouthard's study would give the term "depression" a greater impact in court in relating it to the seriousness of the events of the workplace and the consequences of those events. You would also need to validate the study in court as reliable and professionally acceptable, as no doubt, the defense will question this.

Should you require any further information, please do not hesitate to contact us. We appreciate your expertise, your time, and kind consideration of Mr./Ms. Workplace Victim and we look forward to receiving your report in due course.

Yours sincerely,
Lawyer

Statement of Claim Template

This is only a guide, and you will insert the particular circumstances that apply to your client. This template relates to a policeman who was harassed and bullied in the workplace. The law firm thought he might get about $40,000, but this case actually settled for close to $400,000 (a Supreme Court settlement which was closely watched by the police commissioner). It was settled out of court to avoid the publicity, which would have resulted in an avalanche of similar cases, as bullying was rampant in the police services at that time.

An important part of his rehabilitation was that the young man would study a course at Bond University (a private university)—which should include relocation costs, fees, private tuition, books, materials, living expenses, and so on. The rational was that he was so traumatized and injured in the workplace that he would be required to attend a small private educational facility in order to cope. Look at the fees and expenses at a private university so you can increase your client's payout. Be creative when assessing your client needs for compensation and rehabilitation. As a last word, you can always come down with the compensation but you can never go up—so aim high for compensating your client.

Statement of Claim Guide

1. At all material times, the Defendant was the employer of the Plaintiff.
2. In or about (insert date) the First Plaintiff commenced employment with the Defendant in the ...
3. The Defendant was at all material times capable of suing and being sued and was known as ...
4. At all material times the Plaintiff was acting in the course of his employment.
5. The Plaintiff was sworn into (name of service) and thereafter posted to ... followed by a posting to ...
6. Whilst a member of ... the Plaintiff performed his duties in accordance with directed work policy.
7. It was a term of the contract of employment between the Plaintiff and the Defendant and/or otherwise it was the duty of the Defendant to take all reasonable precautions to avoid the risk of injury to the physical and mental health of the Plaintiff of which the Defendant, its service or agents ought to have been aware.
8. At all material times, it was a term and condition of the contract of employment between the Plaintiff and the Defendant and/or it was otherwise the duty of the Defendant, that it would not without reasonable cause, conduct itself in a manner likely to damage or destroy the relationship of confidence and trust between the parties as the employer and the employee.
9. Further and/or in the alternative, it was the statutory duty of the Defendant to provide the Plaintiff with a safe system of work.

10. At all material time, the servants or agents (or in the service) of the Defendant, were subject to directions issued by the Commissioner of . . . within the meaning of that term as defined by the Police Service Administration Act 1990 (the Act) and as such were subject to act in accordance with the Code of Conduct promulgated by the Commissioner of Police pursuant to section . . . of the Act.

11. As from the . . . day of (date) the Defendant was a "public sector entity" within the meaning of that term as defined by the Public Sector Ethics Act 1994 (the Ethics Act). The Defendant, its servants or agents (or in the service) the Defendant negligently and in breach of their duties, failed to comply with their obligations to the First Plaintiff pursuant to the Ethics Act in that:

    a. The First Plaintiff was not treated with respect
    b. The First Plaintiff was not treated in accordance with ethics principles
    c. The First Plaintiff was not treated in accordance with the Code of Conduct
    d. The (employer) was negligent in not enforcing its obligations as defined in the Code of Conduct.

12. The Plaintiff was required to perform all such tasks as were ordinarily required of him/her at the direction of senior officers.

13. Whilst engaged in duties at . . . the Plaintiff was subject to victimization by the servants and or agents of the Defendant.

14. Particulars of the victimization are:

    a. Regular obscene gestures
    b. Regular obscene remarks
    c. Constant personal insults
    d. On the message board, the letter *p* was regularly placed in front of the Plaintiff's name "Rick."

e. Envelopes addressed to the Plaintiff were regularly defaced with obscenities.

f. The Plaintiff constantly found his files damaged by spilt coffee, rotten fruit squashed on them, torn, or destroyed.

g. The Plaintiff's care was damaged deliberately whilst parked in a police security car park.

h. List all the other acts from the Events Chart

15. In the premises, the Plaintiff suffered psychological and physical injuries. By reasons of these premises, the Plaintiff has suffered loss and damage in that he has suffered stress, vexation, loss of dignity and hurt.

16. In breach of the terms of employment referred to in paragraphs . . . and . . . above and/or alternatively in breach of the duty referred to in paragraphs . . . above, the Defendant failed to provide the First Plaintiff with a safe system of work and in particular:

During the time the Plaintiff was employed by the Defendant, the Defendant failed to provide a safe system, of work for the First Plaintiff in that the Defendant required the First Plaintiff to work under the supervision of and with persons who harassed and unfairly treated and discriminated against the Plaintiff during the carrying out by the First Plaintiff of his duties for the Defendant.

17. As a result of the Defendant's breach of contract and/or breach of duty and/or breach of statutory duty, the Plaintiff has suffered injuries and loss and damage, in particular of which are as follows:

a. A stress related illness
b. A decompensation into an anxiety depressive state
c. An inability to continue working for the Defendant

18. Particulars of the psychological injury are as follows:

a. The Plaintiff has suffered a mental breakdown.
b. The Plaintiff required two years of psychotherapy.
c. The Plaintiff required desensitization and management of stress symptoms.
d. The Plaintiff has undergone pain and suffering. (Describe the physical aspects that were detailed above)

19. Further, in the course of his duties, the Plaintiff was subjected to physical stress and danger by the actions of other members of the . . . whilst stationed at . . .

20. Particulars of the physical injuries and danger are as follows:

a. Co-workers of the Plaintiff tampered with his gun whilst it was stored in the gun locker.
b. List other events from the Events Chart that put your client in danger.

21. In the premises, the Plaintiff has suffered physically.

22. Particulars of the Plaintiff's physical suffering are:

a. The Plaintiff takes prescribed anti-depressant tablets and sedatives.
b. The Plaintiff has sleeping problems.
c. The Plaintiff suffers from dizziness and headaches. (Describe the physical injuries described above).

23. The Plaintiff also suffered humiliation, fear, and a loss of confidence in his co-workers as a result of the aforementioned in number 11.

24. Particulars of the Plaintiff's suffering of humiliation, fear, and a loss of confidence in his co-workers:

a. The Plaintiff is undergoing psychotherapy and has been diagnosed as requiring further psychotherapy for a further . . . years.

25. As a result of the matters aforesaid, the Plaintiff has been rendered unfit for employment and unable to perform work related activities.
26. The Plaintiff has suffered economic loss and damage. Particulars of economic loss suffered will be delivered prior to trial.
27. In the premises, the Plaintiff remains unfit for work.
28. The Plaintiff has suffered a career loss and damage as a result of matters herein before referred to.
29. As a result of the First Plaintiff's said injuries he has experienced the following:

   a. Past economic loss
   b. Is likely to suffer future economic loss
   c. Has suffered, is suffering, and will continue to suffer reduction and loss of amenities of life
   d. Has received medical, psychological, psychiatric, and other treatments and will continue to do so in the future
   e. Has required the assistance of others in many aspects of his day to day living, which assistance it would have been reasonable to obtain at a cost
   f. Has suffered special damages, full details of which will be supplied to the solicitors for the Defendant prior to the trial of this action
   g. Will be at risk of not being able to obtain employment commensurate with his qualifications and training in the future on the open market and will require total retraining in order to re-enter the work force.

30. Defendant had a duty of care to ensure a safe workplace.
31. Defendant was at all material times under a duty of care to the Plaintiff to take reasonable care for the Plaintiff's safety and well being during the course of his employment with the Defendant.

32. The Defendant breached said duty by subjecting the Plaintiff to undue stress at his work in the circumstances hereinafter pleaded.
33. Particulars of negligence:

    a. Complaints by the Plaintiff to . . . (list senior officers/staff) were ignored. Further particulars will be supplied prior to trial. (List everything from the Events Chart when asked for particulars)

34. The injuries suffered by the Plaintiff were reasonably foreseeable.
35. As a result of the stress the Plaintiff was placed under at work, he suffered a breakdown of his emotional and mental processes as a manifestation of a severe stress reaction with the development of a persisting mixed anxiety depressive illness (hereinafter referred to as "the injury").
36. Particulars of the Plaintiff's special damage will be supplied prior to the trial of the action.
37. The Plaintiff has not been able to do any work whatsoever.
38. In the premises the injuries were caused by the negligence of the Defendant, particulars of which are as follows:

    a. Failing to provide the Plaintiff with a system of work that was free from risk of injury
    b. Failing to take any steps to prevent the Plaintiff from sustaining an injury from being placed under undue stress
    c. Failing to take any steps to direct the Defendant's employees to avoid placing the Plaintiff under undue stress
    d. Failing to take any steps to direct the Defendant's employees to remove the Plaintiff from situations of undue stress at work when those situations arose

e. Failing to provide the Plaintiff with counseling and/ or other support and assistance to enable him to cope with his/her stress at work
f. Placing the Plaintiff in situations where he was under increased stress at work
g. Treating the Plaintiff in a harsh and unfair manner at work and during and subsequent complaints by the Plaintiff
h. In rejecting the Plaintiff's grievance complaint without full consideration of it, the Defendant acted harshly, arbitrarily, and unfairly towards the Plaintiff.

39. The Writ of Summons in this action was served on . . . on the . . . day of . . . 20 . . .
AND the Plaintiff claims for breach of contract of employment, breach of duty, negligence and breach of statutory duty:

a. General damages
b. Special damages
c. Interest pursuant to statute at such rate and for such time as this Honorable Court deems meet.

AND the Plaintiff claims:

1. . . . hundred thousand dollars ($ . . .) damages for the breach of duty and negligence.
2. Interest
3. Costs

Dated this . . . day of . . . year

Workplace Bullying/Harassment Horror Cases

A parliamentary inquiry in 2005 heard evidence of suicides, racism, and gang rapes in the Australian armed services. Bullying and harassment appeared to be sanctioned as normal behavior and part of the culture until parents of victims gave evidence at the Senate committee. Bullying in the military is targeted at a specific person/s with actions, words, directions, and implied and real threats to enshrine the power and self-importance of the Machiavellian-like perpetrators.

In March 2004, the Sydney Administrative Appeals Tribunal awarded compensation to a former navy midshipman whom it found had become mentally disabled after being abused at the Australian Defense Force Academy (ADFA). The abuse allegedly included *woofering*, abusing the victim's genitals with a vacuum cleaner, and being hit about the head with other men's genitals, called turkey slapping.

Soldiers from Townsville's Lavarack Barracks dressed as Ku Klux Klan members to intimidate, bully, and taunt soldiers who had dark skin. Dr. Ben Wadham, a former infantry soldier and military policeman in the 2nd/4th Battalion Royal Australian Regiment (2/4 RAR) claimed that bullying, abuse, and sex games are endemic in the Australian army culture, and that the Ku Klux Klan photo was a normal part of everyday behavior in the Australian army.

Soldiers claim that the armor was removed from a dark skinned soldier's flak jacket while serving in East Timor. Furthermore, offensive messages were scrawled on non-white soldiers' equipment. (*Canberra Times* 12 November 2004).

A female naval commander was told she was "fucking useless" and was victimized and bullied on the naval base of HMAS Stirling. The navy told her she would be crucified if she went to the media. She was stood down and her professional and personal reputation destroyed. When she returned to the naval establishment, she was put in charge of the toilets. The navy paid the bully's legal expenses, which came to $377,000. He is still a serving officer (7.30 Report 15 May 2006). The head of defense at the time, Angus Houston, refused to apologize, claiming he never received the request. When the woman went to the media, she was told that she could be sent to a military prison (see *Sydney Morning Herald 17 May 2006.)*

The RAAF failed to protect an airfield defense guard from being bashed after he blew the whistle on drug use and drug abuse at Amberley Air Force Base in Queensland. Instead of receiving praise for blowing the whistle from the RAAF, he received a broken jaw and trauma. He subsequently attempted suicide as a result of the bullying.

Female 31-40: Registered Nurse

I have used long-service/reaction leave for sick leave purposes because I felt ashamed that I was stressed.

I have suffered mental injuries in the workplace but it is too painful and long to describe.

I was forced to supervise a man who is a well-known pedophile. I felt totally repulsed by him. He is white and he exploited black kids. I felt powerless to protect the children from him. I had to leave the job in the end because I could not stand being in his company. I failed the kids but did everything I could to change the situation.

There is no justice. I received no support. Management only looked after them. The union looked after the pedophile because he is very cunning and manipulative. I could not prove he was abusing kids because everyone was too frightened to speak up just because he is a powerful white man. The Aboriginal mob don't trust police and other authorities so it's an impossible situation.

I was victimized and intimidated at work because I was told I was trying to obstruct Aboriginal self-determination by attempting to support Aboriginal people in organizing a meeting by themselves for themselves.

No action was ever taken—only lots of fluffy talk. I was too frightened of legal repercussions through the Public Service Act.

I quit my job and changed professions. I was so pissed off and obviously still am.

Registered symptoms of PTSD

Female 41-50: Enrolled Nurse. Private Hospital

I suffered anxiety, crying at work and insomnia because of workplace psychological distress. Harassed by boss daily. Constantly shouted at. A work colleague attempted suicide as she couldn't take any more.

Female 51-60: Registered Nurse. Large Public Hospital

Constantly put down and yelled to make the bully look good. Threatened to be sued. Constantly put down. I sobbed and sobbed. It was most destroying. There is great mistrust in this workplace. The leader yells at me and intimidates me. I did not report the incident s because I did not have the confidence. How do you put in a grievance if it comes from a top position. My observation is recently I have seen a lot of bullying with the colleague that I work with.

There is a total lack of confidence because of the level of the profession that it (the bullying) comes from. I have recently seen people in tears but there is hopelessness around them. They see the only answer is to resign and work in another health service. They do not have the confidence to go through grievance procedures because the complaint is about their superiors. Is there any way that persons could go to an outside mediator for abuse first?

A work colleague of this subject committed suicide because of workplace bullying intimidation and victimization.

Female 31-40: Registered Nurse. Public Hospital

I am made to lift too heavy objects and am made to feel stupid. I feel the stress of victimization at work contributed to my miscarriage. I reported the incidents but no action was taken.

Registered symptoms of PTSD

Male 31-40: Registered Nurse. Large Public Hospital

Unmanageable work loads. Stress levels not recognized. Victimized because of going to WorkCover and then going on compensation. Forcing me to leave that workplace. I suffered burnout, depression and a mental breakdown. I reported the victimizing incidents but no action was taken. I just had to get on with it. They did not want to know about it.

Female 31-40: Registered Nurse. Large Public Hospital

I knew a person who committed suicide over workplace bullying in this hospital. I am verbally abused by a senior member in from of staff, doctors and patients. A senior member, in front of staff, doctors and patients verbally abuses me. Constant undermining statements are made to me. I'm fed up.

Registered symptoms of PTSD

Male 21-30: Registered Nurse. Large Public Hospital

There is never anyone to report the acts of victimization to. The union representative is unsupportive and unable to assist. Due to victimization, I had decreased productivity, anxiety, depression, panic attacks, low self-esteem and confidence and felt distrustful and resentful.

Registered symptoms of PTSD

Female 41-50: Nurse Manager. Large Public Hospital

I suffer frequent migraines, loss of concentration and am poorly motivated with work issues. I constantly cry when faced with the bully. I had to take Zoloft. I have never taken nerve pills in my life up to this point. A close friend (also a manager) was interrogated and then sacked. I intervened. The allegations made about my friend were false. Information is often not passed on to me or I am not included in meeting about my area of expertise. I am constantly hounded by the Assistant Director of Nursing to do more work, do more study. and put in more hours. This person often changes her mind on tasks allocated and does not let me know. She would also deny authority after verbally ordering work to be commenced. I feel my workplace only plays lip service to the harassment legislation and the workplace health and safety requirements. In the end I resigned as the abuse continued. Since then, many of my co-managers have also left.

Female 31-40: Registered Nurse. Private Aged Care

I get continual e-mails from the supervisor re "grievance procedures." I get no aid from Queensland Health and am told to get over with it. Made to feel incompetent. I am the only registered nurse for 61 residents and there are 2 carers. My distress is caused by the low morale of all the staff and the continual put-downs by the supervisor.

Female 20-30: Registered Nurse. Large Public Hospital

A friend of mine committed suicide because of the victimization that goes on at this hospital. The workplace completely destroyed my self-confidence in myself and in my work situation. I think I would have ended up having a breakdown if I had stayed. One midwife bullied me by giving excessive workloads and undermining me in from of the patients and staff. She was constantly rude and nasty but no in front of witnesses plus a whole lot of other stuff that's hard to describe. No action was taken. I told the CNC and the supervisor. They said I wasn't the only one but I had to use a grievance procedure. I was not emotionally able to go through with this.

Female 51-60: Registered Nurse. Aged Persons Home

I was the Queensland Nurses' Union representative but I had to resign because the Director of Nursing victimized me and caused the staff to isolate me. She wanted to know why I considered her actions insensitive.

I felt devalued.

I felt an inability to cope.

I was distrustful and didn't wish to return to work following a specific incident during a general staff meeting where attempts were made to discredit me.

I suffered public humiliation. I was in shock and disbelief, then anger and later feelings of rejection, alienation and poor self-esteem.

I developed anxiety. My immune system was lowered resulting in sore throat, headaches, sinus, thrush and chest infection.

Certain triggers are still present to undermine my health.

The Director of Nursing is the rehabilitation coordinator who discredited me at staff meetings.

I attempted to overcome my medical condition regarding stress and anxiety but on return to work, there was no change in their behavior.

Documentation is never completed.

I am told *I pay you to be busy.*

It's the nature of the industry.

Others have left because of victimization.

There is no training on bullying.

Annual leave is not granted with requested. Favorites always get theirs.

I lost pay because of victimization.

There seems to be a "culture of intimidation/harassment" where many at work do not realize it is happening or that it is unacceptable. It occurs at all levels and is not isolated to a few.

Both psychologists I saw said that it was rampant in aged care health.

There is a "kick the dog" syndrome from the Director of Nursing downwards with many aged care facilities.

Desperately need to have something available and easily accessible and non-threatening to assist people going through the early stages of bullying.

I did a lot of work on my own and was determined to get back to work.

Registered many of the symptoms of PTSD

Female 41-50: Enrolled Nurse. Public Aged Care

Had to leave the workplace area but still on the premises due to a lack of control.

Thought I may do harm to the person doing the bullying.

Not wanting to work.

Nauseated at the thought of entering the building.

Management constantly derides staff efforts at bringing safety issues to their attention.

Staff are not supported.

Management always ask other staff and visitors what the staff member did to the person who abused or attacked them.

They never believe their staff. The staff is always at fault— especially when management is the ones doing it—abusing the patients.

I am screamed at and threatened with dismissal all the time.

I am told the other staff hate working with me and that they are taking sick leave rather than work with me.

I can't report the incidents as the victimization and intimidation is done by management who are careful to make sure that there are no witnesses.

No representation (by the union) is allowed.

Female 51-60: Registered Nurse. Private Hospital

I am experienced in gerontology (geriatrics) and aged and palliative nursing care. When I worked in a large public hospital, I began an educational program to update my skills. However,

I found the clinical nurse both aggressive and intimidating. My confidence began to fade as the clinical nurse constantly found fault with me.

She did not confront me directly with the issues she found in my work.

She would arrange for the nurse educator to do this. I endured snide remarks made within my hearing but done in such a way that I could not complain.

She treated me in a derisive way in front of other staff members, particularly those who were less qualified than me.

Every day was a nightmare and I dreaded going to work. I became very depressed and had to commence on anti-depressants. I was unable to concentrate. I confided in the nurse educator who then arranged for me to see the clinical psychologist within the hospital.

Yet the victimization continued and I began to feel suicidal.

The final straw was my appraisal. This clinical nurse told me that she could not find one positive thing to say about me. I retaliated with a formal letter to her rejecting the appraisal. I contacted the union but I found little support. They had, I was told, addressed the issue of sexual harassment, but not bullying.

Finally I decided to resign as I felt I had no other alternative. When I approached the DON (Director of Nursing) she has these words to say. "It's better that you go back into aged care. If you get bored you can always take up tapestry."

Such is the opinion that some nurses have in regards to those who chose to care for elderly people. Hopefully that DON will find herself in an aged care facility one day and then realize we don't' have time to become bored.

NOW—Go back to the Events Chart (EC) and copy it for your client. Make sure your client completes the EC on a daily basis in the workplace so a pattern of behavior emerges. List all medications and times when taking the medications.

You will require professionals. The Private Group Pty Ltd is an excellent organization with professional investigators who specialize in all types of investigations. The Private Group is based in Australia and is operational worldwide. Phone 1399 966 103 or +61 7 47788970.

With the exciting advancements in neuroscience and brain imaging, investigate these possibilities with your client's psychologist and psychiatrist. Injuries such as depression can be identified and proved with modern advances in neuroscience.

References

Australian Public Service Commission: "Eliminating workplace harassment guidelines."

Bowie, V. 2002. Defining violence at work: A new typology.

Gill, M., Fisher, B., and Bowie, V. (eds) (2002), *Violence At Work: Causes, Patterns and Prevention. Cullompton,* UK: Wilan.

Chambers 21st Century Dictionary (2004). Chambers AAT, Australia. 2004.

Cocchiarella L & Andersson G.B.J 2001. *Guides to the Evaluation of Permanent Impairment*, 5th ed., USA. American Medical Association Press.

Crabtree, M. 1994. "Occupational Health and Safety." *Australian Business Law Review, 22.*

Diagnostic and Statistical Manual of Mental Disorders 1994 4th ed. American Psychiatric Association 1400 k Street, N.W., Washington DC 20005.

Einarsen, S. 1998. "Dealing with bullying at work: The Norwegian lesson." Paper presented at the Bullying at Work 1998 Research Update Conference, Staffordshire University Business School.

Einarsen, S., and A Skogstad,. (1996). "Bullying at Work: Epidemiological findings in public and private organizations." *European Journal of Work and Organizational Psychology* 5 (2).

Fisse, B., and J Braithwaite. (1988). "The Allocation of Responsibility for Corporate Crime: Individualism, Collectivism and Accountability." *Sydney Law Review* 11.

Goodwin, S.A., A, Gubin, S.T. Fiske, and V. Y. Yzerbyt. 2000. "Power Can Bias Impression Processes: Stereotyping Subordinates by Default and by Design." *Group Processes & Intergroup Relations 3*.

Greenberg, D. 2009. *Stroud's Judicial Dictionary,* UK. Sweet and Maxwell.

Gupta, R. K., R. Kumar and S. Kasper. 2002. "Physical Signs in Psychiatry: A step towards evidence based medicine." *International Journal of Psychiatry in Clinical Practice,* 6 (2).

Hall, D. R. 1982. "Commonwealth Controls with Respect to Victimization of Employees." *Australian Law Journal* 56.

Hutchinson, M., M. Vickers, D. Jackson, and L. Wilkes. 2010. "Bullying as circuits of power." *Administrative Theory & Praxis* 32 (1).

Kendell, R. 1975. "Concept of Disease and its Implications for Psychiatry." *British Medical Journal* 127.

Kutas, M. and K. D. Federmeier. 1998. "Minding the body." *Psychophysiology* 35.

Leymann, H. 1990. "Mobbing and psychological terror at workplaces." *Violence and Victims* 5 (2).

Lovell, B. L. and R. T. Lee. 2011 "Impact of workplace bullying on emotional and physical well-being: A longitudinal collective case study." *Journal of Aggression, Maltreatment & Trauma* 20 (3).

Heinz, L. 1994. *"Explanation of the Operation of the LIPT Questionnaire,"* (Leymann Inventory of Psychological Terror), translated from the original German by Helga Zimmermann, consulting psychologist, Brisbane.

Liefooghe, A. and K. M. Davey. 2010. "The language and organization of bullying at work." *Administrative Theory and Praxis,* 32 (1).

Lubinski, R. 1994. Burnout. *Issues in Speech-Language Pathology and Audiology,* ed. R. Lubinski and C. Frattali California, Singular Publishing Group Inc.

Mann, R. 1996. "Psychological Abuse in the Workplace." Developed from Biderman's Chart of Coercion in Amnesty International, *Report on Torture,* London: Duckworth. 1975.

Maslach, C. 1982. *Burnout: the cost of caring,* New Jersey: Prentice-Hall.

O'Keene, V. 2000. "Evolving model of depression as an expression of multiple interacting factors." *British Journal of Psychiatry* 177.

Rawls, J. 1971. *A Theory of Justice.* Cambridge, Massachusetts: Harvard University Press.

Rowell, P.A. 2005. "Being a 'target' at work." *Journal of Nursing Management,* 35.

Sanders, R.D. and M. S. Keshavan. 1998. "The neurologic examination in adult psychiatry: from soft signs to hard science." *Journal of Neuropsychiatry and Clinical Neuroscience,* 10.

Schneid, Thomas D. and Michael S. Schumann. 1997. *Legal Liability,* Maryland: Aspen Publications.

Scrignar, C. B. 1997. *Post Traumatic Stress Disorder, Psychiatry in Court,* 2nd ed. Sydney: Hawkins Press.

Stouthard M. 1997. *Disability Weights for Diseases.* Netherlands: Department of Public Health.

Taber's Cyclopedic Medical Dictionary 1993. 17th ed., Philadelphia: F. A. Davis and Company.

United Nations International Covenant on Economic, Social and Cultural Rights ICESCR).

Vickers, M. 2010. "Symposium: Bullying, mobbing and violence in organizational life." *Administrative Theory & Praxis,* 32 (1).

Von Korff, M. and G. Simon. 1996. "The Relationship Between Pain and Depression:" *British Journal of Psychiatry,* 168.

Wilkie, W. 1996. *Bullying From Backyard to Boardroom,* Sydney: Millennium Books.

World Health Organization. 1997. *Prevention of Violence: Public Health Priority,* WHO World Health Assembly, Resolution

49.25 of 25 May 1996. Document EB/99/INF. Doc/3 of 7 January 1997.

Wynne, R., N. Clarkin, T. Cox and A. Griffiths. 1996. *Guidance on the Prevention of Violence at Work,* Luxembourg: European Commission DG-V.

Zegans, L. S. 1982. Stress and the development of somatic disorders, *Handbook of stress: Theoretical and clinical aspects,* L. Goldberger, and S. Breznitz, eds New York: Free Press.

Cases

Adeels Palace Pty Ltd v Anthony Moubarak (2009) 239 CLR 420

Ahern v R (1988) 62 ALJR 440

Arnold v Midwest Radio Ltd [1999] QCA 20

Attorney General's Department v K [2010] NSWWCCPD 76

Auckland Provincial District Local Authorities v Mt Albert City Council (1989) 2 NZILR 651

Austin v Director-General of Education (1994) 10 NSWCR 373

Bahatia v State Rail Authority (NSW) 14 NSWCCR 568

Baltic Shipping Co. v Dillon [1992-93] 176 CLR 344

Barber v Somerset County Council [2004] 1 WLR 1089

Batiste v State of Queensland (2002) 2QdR 119

Bliss v South East Thames Health Authority (1987) ICR 700

Blyth v Birmingham Co (1856) 11 Exch. 781

Bostik (Aust) Pty Ltd v Gorgevski (No 1) [1992] 41 IR 452

Bourhill v Young [1943] AC 92

Brooks v Comcare (1995) 38 ALD 612

Carlisle v Council of the Shire of Kilkivan and Brietkreutz Briekreutz (1995) Qld District Court No. 2/12/1995

Charles R Davidson & Co v McRobb [1918] AC 304

Chugg v Pacific Dunlop Ltd (1990) 170 CLR 249

Comcare v Moori (1996) 132 ALR 690

Wyong Shire Council v Shirt (1980) 146 CLR

Cresswell v The Board of England Revenue (1984) 2 All ER 713

Crimmins v Stevedoring Industry Finance Committee (1999) 74 ALJR 1

David v Britannic Merthyn Co [1909] 2 KB 164

De Romanis v Sibraa [1977] 2 NSWLR 264

Di Barrista v Comcare (1996) AAT unreported No. V94/25

Doherty v NSW [2010] NSWSC 450

Donoghue v Stevenson [1932] AC 562

Earl v Slater & Wheeler Ltd (1973) 1 All ER 145

Farrelly v Qantas Airways Ltd (2001) 22 NSWCCR 331

Federal Broom Co. Pty Ltd v Semlitch (1964) 110 CLR 626

Filliter v Phippard (1847) 11 QB 347

Gardiner v Motherwell Machinery and Scrap Co Ltd [1961] 1 WLR 1424

Grant v Australian Knitting Mills Ltd [1936] AC 85

Hamilton v Nuroof (WA) Pty Ltd (1956) 96 CLR 15

Hamilton v Whitehead (1988) 82 ALR 626

Haneef and Dept Immigration (The Tribunal) 48 AR 153

Hawthorne v Thiess Contractors Pty Ltd [2001] 401 QCA 223

Hoffmueller v Commonwealth [1981] 54 FLR 48

Humphrey Earl Ltd v Speechley (1951) 84 CLR 126

Hungerfords v Walker (1989) 63 ALJ 210.

Jackson v Work Directions Australia Pty Ltd (1998) 17 NSWCCR 70

Jaensch v Coffey (1984) 156 CLR 549

John L Pty Ltd v Attorney General (NSW) (1987) 163 CLR 508

Johnson v Miller (1937) 59 CLR 467

Jones v Dunkel [1958-59] 101 CLR 298

Kennedy Cleaning Services Pty Ltd v Petkoska (2000) 74 ALR 626

Kirk v Industrial Court (NSW) (2010) 239 CLR 531

Koehler v Cerebos (Australia Pty Ltd) [2005] HCA 15

Kondis v State Transport Authority (1984) 154 CLR 672

Lennard's Supermarkets Ltd v Asiatic Petroleum Co Ltd [1915] AC 705

March v E & MH Stramare Pty Ltd (1991) 171 CLR 506

McKernan v Fraser (1931) 46 CLR 343

McKierman v Manhire (1977) 17 SASR 571

McLean v Tedman (1985) 155 CLR 306

Metropolitan Gas Co v City of Melbourne (1924) 35 CLR 186

Mobb v King Island Council (1994) unreported, Industrial Relations Court of Australia, VI 2246

Mogul SS Co Ltd v McGregor, Gow & Co (1892) AC 25

Mt Isa Mines v Hopper [1997] EQC 92-879

Mt Isa Mines Limited v Pusey (1971) 125 CLR 383

NSW v Fahy [2007] 232 CLR 486

Nimmo v Alexander Cowan & Sons Ltd [1968] AC 107

Opera House Investments Pty Ltd v Devon Buildings Pty Ltd. (1936) 55 CLR 110

Page v Smith [1996] 1 AC 155

Paradis v R (1934) 61 CCC 184

Parnell (1881) 14 Cox CC 508

Perkins v Grace Worldwide (Aust) Pty Ltd (1997) 72 IR 18

Post Office v Roberts (1980) IRLR 347

Printing Industry Employees Union of Australia v Jackson & O'Sullivan Pty Ltd (1958) 1 FLR 175

Pyne v Wilkenfield (1981) 26 SASR 441

Queensland Corrective Services v Gallagher (1998) QCA 426

Quinn v Leathem (1901) AC 495

Rahman v Arearose Ltd [2001] QB 351

R v Goodall (1975) 11 SASR 94 at 101

R v Jones (1830) 110 ER 485

Rogers v Brambles Australia Ltd (1989) 1 Qld R 218

Shields v Warringarri Aboriginal Corporation [2009] FWA 860

Sinnott v F J Trousers Pty Ltd [2000] VSC 124

Sorrell v Smith [1925] AC 700

State of New South Wales v Seedman [2000] NSW CA 119

Stewart v NSW Police Service (1998) 17 NSWCCR 202

Tame v New South Wales [2002] 211 CLR 317

Tesco Supermarkets Ltd v Nattrass [1972] AC 153

Thazine-Ayr v WorkCover NSW (1995) 12 NSWCCR 304

Thom v Sinclair [1917] AC 127

Tripodi v R (1961) 104 CLR 1

Tymshare Inc v Covell 727 F2d 1145 (1984)

Legislation

Civil Liability Act 2002 (NSW)
Fair Work Act 2009 (Cth)
Freedom of Information Act 1989 (ACT)
Freedom of Information Act 1982 (Cth)
Law Reform (Vicarious Liability) Act 1983 (NSW)
Occupational Health and Safety Act 1989 (ACT)
Occupational Health and Safety Act (Cth) 2000
Occupational Health and Safety Act (NSW)
Occupational Health, Safety and Welfare Act 1986 (SA)
Occupational Health and Safety Act 1985 (Vic)
Occupational Health and Safety Act 2004 (Vic)
Occupational Safety and Health Act 1984 (WA)
Police Service Administration Act (Qld) 1990
Public Health Service Act (Sweden), Act 1985. (Svensk forfattningssaamling, 1985.)
Public Sector Ethics Act 1994
Safety Rehabilitation and Compensation Act (Cth) 1988
Work Health Act NT
Work Environment Act Sweden 1993
Workers Compensation Act 1988
World Health Organization Act 1947 (Cth)
Working Environment Act Netherlands 1980
Model Work Health and Safety Act 2010
Workplace Health and Safety Act 2009 (NT)
Workplace Health and Safety Act 1995 (Qld)
Workplace Health and Safety Act 1995 (Tas)

Workplace Injury Management and Workers Compensation Act 1998
Workplace Relations Act 1996 (Cth)
Work Safety Act 2008 (ACT)
Work Environment Act (Sweden) 1977